Editor-in-Chief and Founder:
  Lyndon H. LaRouche, Jr.
Editorial Board: *Lyndon H. LaRouche, Jr. , Helga
  Zepp-LaRouche, Robert Ingraham, Tony
  Papert, Gerald Rose, Dennis Small, Jeffrey
  Steinberg, William Wertz*
Co-Editors: *Robert Ingraham, Tony Papert*
Managing Editor: *Nancy Spannaus*
Technology: *Marsha Freeman*
Books: *Katherine Notley*
Ebooks: *Richard Burden*
Graphics: *Alan Yue*
Photos: *Stuart Lewis*
Circulation Manager: *Stanley Ezrol*

INTELLIGENCE DIRECTORS
Counterintelligence: *Jeffrey Steinberg, Michele
  Steinberg*
Economics: *John Hoefle, Marcia Merry Baker,
  Paul Gallagher*
History: *Anton Chaitkin*
Ibero-America: *Dennis Small*
Russia and Eastern Europe: *Rachel Douglas*
United States: *Debra Freeman*

INTERNATIONAL BUREAUS
Bogotá: *Miriam Redondo*
Berlin: *Rainer Apel*
Copenhagen: *Tom Gillesberg*
Houston: *Harley Schlanger*
Lima: *Sara Madueño*
Melbourne: *Robert Barwick*
Mexico City: *Gerardo Castilleja Chávez*
New Delhi: *Ramtanu Maitra*
Paris: *Christine Bierre*
Stockholm: *Ulf Sandmark*
United Nations, N.Y.C.: *Leni Rubinstein*
Washington, D.C.: *William Jones*
Wiesbaden: *Göran Haglund*

ON THE WEB
e-mail: eirns@larouchepub.com
www.larouchepub.com
www.executiveintelligencereview.com
www.larouchepub.com/eiw
Webmaster: *John Sigerson*
Assistant Webmaster: *George Hollis*
Editor, Arabic-language edition: *Hussein Askary*

EIR (ISSN 0273-6314) *is published weekly
(50 issues), by EIR News Service, Inc.,
P.O. Box 17390, Washington, D.C. 20041-0390.
(703) 297-8434*

European Headquarters: *E.I.R. GmbH, Postfach
Bahnstrasse 9a, D-65205, Wiesbaden, Germany
Tel: 49-611-73650
Homepage: http://www.eir.de
e-mail: info@eir.de
Director: Georg Neudecker*

Montreal, Canada: 514-461-1557
eir@eircanada.ca

Denmark: EIR - Danmark, Sankt Knuds Vej 11,
basement left, DK-1903 Frederiksberg, Denmark.
Tel.: +45 35 43 60 40, Fax: +45 35 43 87 57. e-mail:
eirdk@hotmail.com.

Mexico City: EIR, Sor Juana Inés de la Cruz 242-2
Col. Agricultura C.P. 11360
Delegación M. Hidalgo, México D.F.
Tel. (5525) 5318-2301
eirmexico@gmail.com

Copyright: ©2017 EIR News Service. All rights
reserved. Reproduction in whole or in part without
permission strictly prohibited.

Canada Post Publication Sales Agreement
#40683579

Postmaster: Send all address changes to *EIR*, P.O.
Box 17390, Washington, D.C. 20041-0390.

Signed articles in *EIR* represent the views of the authors,
and not necessarily those of the Editorial Board.

There Was
No Russian Hack

ZEPP-LAROUCHE ON FRIDAY WEBCAST

Wake Up Americans!
Your Constitution Is Being Trashed!

Live from Germany, Helga Zepp-LaRouche was the guest on the LaRouche PAC Friday Webcast of Aug. 4. This transcript has been edited.

Host Jason Ross: Hi there! This is Friday, August 4, 2017, and you are joining us for our regular Friday Webcast here at larouchepac.com. I'm Jason Ross—I'll be the host today—and I'm very happy that this week, we are joined by special guest Helga Zepp-LaRouche, who is on with us via video from Germany. Hi there, Helga.

Helga Zepp-LaRouche: Hello. How are you?

Ross: Good! For the show today, as a brief bit of set-up before we get to Helga, this week we saw Donald Trump sign the sanctions bill that had been passed by the House and the Senate—H.R. 3364—which targets Iran, North Korea, and Russia with sanctions. Part of this bill claims, as a given, that Russia interfered with the U.S. election; part of the bill says that the United States will never recognize Crimea as part of Russia; and it would tie the President's hands in having foreign policy actions passed by the House and the Senate rather than through the Executive Branch. Donald Trump signed the bill this week, issuing a signing statement about the parts of the bill that he finds to be unconstitutional. Trump tweeted just yesterday that "Our relationship with Russia is at an all-time and dangerous low. A very dangerous low. You can thank Congress for this."

Russia responded by calling for the expulsion of a certain number of U.S. diplomats to reach the level of Russian diplomats in the United States; something similar to what President Obama had done with Russian diplomats and Russian diplomatic property. What this means overall, is that it's really increasing the pressure on U.S.-Russian relations, and making it very difficult for Trump to follow through on one of his campaign promises, which was the potential of reaching a detente with Russia. As he had famously said, "It's not bad to get along with Russia; that's a good thing."

So, Helga, I'd like to bring you on to provide your view of this. I know that your husband, Lyndon LaRouche, has said that if this coup against Trump succeeds, this puts the threat of nuclear war very much on the table. Could you tell us your view of the situation?

Zepp-LaRouche: Yes. I think this is not just a Senate vote, or a Congress vote. This is about the President in American history since its founding. Because it completely overturns the American Constitution, which gives the power to define foreign policy to the President, and the Constitution has a separation of powers. Now, under the bill that was voted, after the Congress and the Senate voted by an overwhelming majority to impose sanctions, if President Trump wanted to undo that, he would supposedly have to send a letter to the Congress, and the Congress would have to respond in 30 days to either approve it or oppose it.

That is Congress hijacking the power to define foreign policy from the President! I think the American people had better wake up to the fact that what is being taken away is the American Constitution. I would think that every American patriot who loves America—and I know the American people are generally very patriotic—they have to understand this moment. Because they just can not let this go. It has so many implications.

The VIPS Memorandum

My husband, Lyndon LaRouche, said that if this is allowed to stick, then we are back to the immediate confrontation against Russia— and also China—as we were with the Obama administration and the control of the neocons, who had controlled United States policy for two terms of George W. Bush and two terms of Obama. It was these neocons who were completely upset that somebody not belonging to the system—like Donald Trump—won the election.

I remember very well that on the 21st of January, the British weekly magazine, *The Spectator*, had a headline saying, it's just a question of whether Trump will be gotten out of office by impeachment, by a coup, or by assassination. The motion towards impeachment is fully under way, as you know. It has just been revealed that the special counsel, Robert Mueller, has a grand jury, which was supposed to be secret, but a leaker again leaked it to *The Guardian* and other media. So the aim there is clearly to advocate some story showing ties of Trump or his team to Russia.

Now let me just be very emphatic. The truth about this matter has to be gotten out. It is historically of the highest significance that the organization of the VIPS— the Veteran Intelligence Professionals for Sanity— former high-ranking intelligence officials from various intelligence agencies of the United States, about a week ago addressed a memorandum to President Trump in which they established, based on their indisputable expertise, forensic evidence that there was no Russian hack. Instead, there was insider leaking; someone downloaded the data from the DNC computers and then masqueraded the whole affair as if it had been done by the Russians.

To investigate this and to examine these findings in the VIPS memorandum—that is the most important way to derail this coup. Rep. Dana Rohrabacher (R-CA) has already commented on the VIPS memorandum. I think we must mobilize the American population to demand that the Congress invite the VIPS representatives to testify, to present their evidence, and indeed support the efforts of such people as Congressman Devin Nunes (R-CA), who is investigating who did the unmasking, who are the leakers. Senator Grassley's ef-forts to do likewise must be supported. In general, I think this Congress has completely discredited itself. The approval rating of the Congress right now, according to the latest polls, is just 10%; I think this is also an historic low.

The British Empire Is the Conspiracy

But I think it now depends on the American people; and you should find all kinds of organizations and institutions representing the people, backing up President Trump. Justice has to be done; the leakers have to be investigated; and the truth has to be re-established. This is of the highest strategic importance. This is not just an internal American affair—I think the Russian characterizations, that this is an internal fight, are not correct. I think this is something much more sinister.

The former weapons inspector in Iraq, Scott Ritter, who was a weapons inspector during the Iraq War, made a very profound characterization. He said, you have complete unison in the U.S. media, the FBI, and other U.S. intelligence agencies, and near unanimity in both houses of Congress; how do you get such complete—in German you would say *Gleichschaltung*— how do you get such a completely univocal performance? Ritter raises the question that this points to a much broader conspiracy going on in American society. I know that people normally get completely unnerved when you mention the word "conspiracy," but I don't think there is another word to characterize what is happening.

You have what people nowadays call the "Deep State" trying to undo the election of an American President, but you have the British role in all of this. I think that there is an effort by the British Empire, having re-established control over U.S. institutions, to go back to what we had once with the neocons in 1992—the Wolfowitz Doctrine that the United States should never allow another country or another group of countries to bypass the military-political or military power of the United States. Now, that was the coup of the neocons after the collapse of the Soviet Union, and they proceeded to try to establish a unipolar world. I think that is exactly expressed in what the Congress did with the sanctions, and by implication it means going back to the confrontation with Russia, and naturally the Thucydides trap in the relationship with China.

This is the warpath. It has incredible implications. I just want to mention a couple of them. First of all, Rus-

U.S. Senate votes on bill targeting Iran, North Korea, and Russia with sanctions.

sian Prime Minister Medvedev reacted much more sharply than President Putin. He said this ends the hope for an improvement in the relationship between the United States and Russia. Then there were various commentaries in Chinese publications that offered China's help to Russia against the effects of the sanctions and also said this will just mean a much closer relationship between Russia and China, and that together we will have deterrence against the United States. Now that is not what the Chinese want; they have offered cooperation, for the United States to join the Belt and Road Initiative, but that is what it leads to.

Russia Sanctions a Dangerous Boomerang

There are two other side-effects of this. One is the relationship with Europe, because the sanctions primarily target Russian natural gas delivery and the idea of building another pipeline, Nord Stream 2, which Germany needs, because the oil supply from Saudi Arabia, the Middle East, is very tricky because of the unstable situation there. The oil reserves in the North Sea are being depleted. But because the United States insists that it has extraterritorial command, obviously the sanctions will hit all firms that produce materials or perform construction work for any energy project with the Russians. This is completely impossible. It will also target, for example, European investors in the United States: If they do business with Russia, they could be expropriated in the United States, or their capital frozen, or the like. This is causing havoc.

The European Union and the German government have already said that they will consider countermeasures, that this may lead to trade war. Amazingly, one spokesman in a leading think tank that is close to the German government has just said this will backfire, because why should countries which are targetted by the sanctions help to implement them? So, he predicts that this will be a boomerang for the Americans; but naturally, a very dangerous one. Also, various German industrial associations came out and said this is completely unacceptable.

More fundamentally, it brings up the question of international law. Why would the United States think that U.S. law can be applied all over the world? This is a violation of international law, and therefore this is an unprecedented crisis. It has, as I said, implications for the American Constitution, for international law, for the relationship with Russia and China; it can break apart the alliance with Europe for the first time. So, I think people really must understand, this must be undone.

Ross: Could you say more for our viewers about what you see as the limitations of the "Deep State" or Cold War idea? In other words, what is really pushing this opposition to cooperation with Russia and what can we do about it?

Financial Blow-Out, Nuclear Extinction

Zepp-LaRouche: I think it is a remnant of geopolitics. Geopolitics is the idea that a group of nations, or one nation which has a fundamental interest against another nation or another group of nations, and if need be, can fight for this with wars of aggression. It was that thinking which led to two world wars in the 20th Century, and obviously, if we don't overcome this in the age of thermonuclear weapons, what we are talking about is the danger of extinction of the human race if it comes to war. We are much closer to this than most people even wish to recognize.

When the Soviet Union disintegrated between 1989

and 1991, there was the possibility to have a lasting, peaceful order. Communism had been defeated, and we proposed at that time the Eurasian Land-Bridge; we were already calling it the New Silk Road. It was the idea of establishing a new paradigm of cooperation in the interest of all participating countries. That policy would have changed the course of history. But at that time there was Margaret Thatcher, and you had Bush, Sr., and Mitterrand.

They decided to prevent Russia from ever coming up again—to reduce the Soviet Union, which was a superpower, to a Russia which would just be a raw materials-producing Third World country. They decided that, instead of having a world order of peace, let's go back to the old Anglo-American policy of running the world as an empire; let's impose a unipolar order on the world. That was the policy of the 1990s, of the early 2000s; it was the idea of ruling through regime change, color revolution. This was the policy of the wars based on lies in Afghanistan, Iraq, the murder of Qaddafi; these policies have destroyed the Middle East. They have caused the refugee crisis; they almost triggered the collapse of the European Union, because there is no union, as became clear in the course of the refugee crisis.

So this policy is now about to explode. Alan Greenspan, of all people—the person who again and again warned of irrational exuberance—just came out and said there is another bond bubble blow-out coming, and it will trigger a collapse of the stock market. This empire is collapsing, and that is why I think there is such desperation to prevent the rise of China; even though China has offered a completely different model, not based on geopolitics but based on "win-win" cooperation, in which all nations cooperating with the New Silk Road Belt and Road Initiative would profit.

Defend the American Revolution!

I think what's really in question here is, do we go back to the British Empire? And people who know American history, know very well that the British Empire never gave up the idea of reconquering the United States. George III lost his marbles at the time of the American Revolution, and the British tried to win America back—first in the War of 1812, then in the Civil War, in which the British Empire was allied with the Confederacy. They financed the Confederacy through the East Coast banks. Then after that, the British realized it could not be done militarily, so then they tried to subvert the American establishment and persuade the leading American families to run the world as an empire based on the Anglo-American special relationship.

If you look at the whole operation against Trump, which really started long before Trump had won the election—it was British Intelligence which started the dossiers fabricating the intelligence. But it was then helped by the U.S. intelligence agencies, whose structure still came from the Obama period. "Deep State" is too short a formulation, because it does not express that this is a British coup. The collusion is not with Russia; the collusion is with this British Empire. Americans have to understand that their entire revolution is at stake; the Constitution—which is still one of the most fantastic documents in terms of constitutions in the world—is in total danger. It is already taken over, and the American people must undo that.

EIR Contents

www.larouchepub.com Volume 44, Number 32, August 11, 2017

Cover This Week

U.S. RUSSIA SANCTIONS

Sanctions: A Coup vs. U.S. Constitution; Germany Must Defend Its Own Interests!

by Helga Zepp-LaRouche, chairwoman of the German political party, Civil Rights Movement Solidarity (BüSo)

Aug. 5—The near-lockstep votes by both houses of the U.S. Congress for new sanctions against Russia (as well as Iran and North Korea) represent an unprecedented scandal, which has game-changing implications on several levels. First, they are a coup against the American Constitution and a reckless attack on America's European "allies." Second, they put a strategic confrontation with Russia and China—which Trump sought to surmount—back on the agenda. And third, they are a violation of international law, because they assert the claim of extraterritoriality for U.S. legislation. It is high time for the rest of the world to learn how to defend its own interests, which can only lie on a totally different political level.

President Trump signed the sanctions bill into law while stating that it included unconstitutional provisions, which he will not implement. Obviously, Trump did not want to face the embarrassment of having the Congress override his veto with a vote far greater than the necessary two-thirds majority. The House of Representatives had voted 419 to 3, and the Senate 98 to 2, for the sanctions bill.

But this legislation represents nothing less than a coup against the United States Constitution of 1787, which gives the President the exclusive power to define relations with other countries. The sanctions law is designed to prevent the President from ever lifting lifting the sanctions. Practically speaking, Trump must now send a formal request for lifting sanctions to the Congress, which would then decide yea or nay within 30 days—something which has very dim prospects, given the majorities just demonstrated. Thus the Congress has virtually seized the Presidential power of making foreign policy, and at the same time has abrogated the constitutional separation of powers between the Executive, Legislative, and Judicial branches, on a decisive matter.

Apparently it took days for the relevant circles in Germany and Europe to recover from the shock of realizing that this legislation also constitutes a violation of international law by the U.S. Congress—by claiming that American laws are applicable extraterritorially, that is, worldwide—since it represents, this time, a total broadside against the existential interests of the European "allies" and "friends" of the United States, namely against their energy security. And, if they were to think about it even more deeply, they would realize that it also affects the question of war and peace in the age of thermonuclear weapons. The new law hits German industry in conditions under which it has al-

The U.S. Capitol, seat of the Congress.

ready suffered for years from the anti-Russia sanctions of the Obama Administration—some firms to the point of bankruptcy—while the volume of U.S. exports to Russia has been increasing over the same time period.

Germany and China React

The new sanctions law threatens punitive measures against companies involved in the Nord Stream 2 (Baltic Sea) pipeline and other Russian energy projects, and thus threatens the suppliers of all the materials needed for construction, and also threatens all the production and service companies, these companys' executives, and the U.S. business of these companies. Spokesmen for the Mechanical Engineering Industry Association (VDMA) and the German Chambers of Industry and Commerce (DIHK) have protested against the

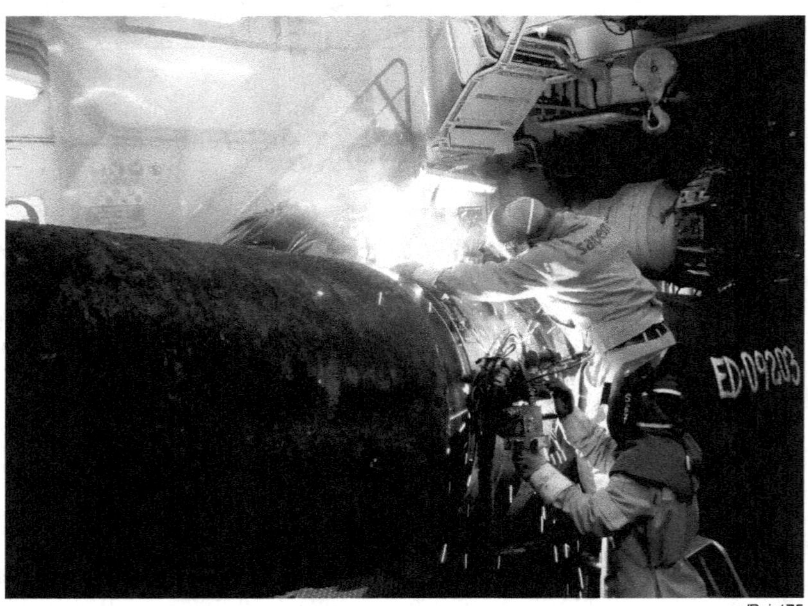

cc/Bair175

Welding pipe segments together for Nord Stream 1 on the Castoro Sei pipelaying vessel, 2011.

sanctions, and demanded a "red line" from the German government, beyond which the effects of the new sanctions law would not be able to reach. That is likely to prove difficult.

Although Foreign Minister Sigmar Gabriel denounced the United States for trying to force Europe to import American liquefied gas (produced by fracking) and Economics Minister Brigitte Zypries condemned the sanctions as a violation of international law, there is a wide array of quislings within the CDU who, for the sake of their Atlanticist careers, would rather sell their grandmothers than defend the national interest.

The German government's policy of synchronizing its reaction to the U.S. sanctions with the European Union (EU) may also come to nothing, given the lack of unity within the EU. On the other hand, Poland and the Baltic states oppose the Nord Stream 2 pipeline, and are willing instruments of Anglo-American manipulations all too often when it comes to Russia. In light of the failed energy transition (to a low-carbon Greeny policy), and the diesel and automakers' cartel scandals, German industry is now coming close to the end of its resources.

Obviously China has realized that the same forces that are responsible for the lockstep vote in the U.S. Congress to impose the new sanctions against Russia, are also reckless enough in their pursuit of a unipolar utopia to fall into the much-cited "Thucydides trap" mentality against China. Several Chinese spokesmen and media outlets have recently announced that China will help Russia manage the economic consequences of the sanctions to its economy, and will also, if need be, support Russia in the event of a crash of the financial system. They point out that China and Russia—whose relationship is the best it has ever been—will deepen their strategic partnership even further, which, under the circumstances, acts as an added deterrent against any potential attack on one or the other in whatever way, including militarily.

As early as Jan. 21, the British weekly magazine *The Spectator* published an article speculating whether President Trump would be removed from office before his term is up—through impeachment, a coup, or assassination. With the unprecedented Congressional vote, the coup is underway. Special Prosecutor Robert Mueller, formerly head of the FBI, and the whole FBI, are currently being called upon to fabricate "evidence" of secret agreements between Putin and Trump, which would then be used to impeach President Trump. Throughout American history, a whole slew of U.S. Presidents have been murdered as part of geopolitical conspiracies; this gives cause for concern that the third option envisaged by *The Spectator* is by no means to be excluded.

What can Germany do in the face of this highly dangerous situation? Several things. First, the current hysteria against Russia rests on two "narratives," both of which lack any foundation in truth; the identification of the real situation in these two cases would discredit or refute the current hype.

Get the Truth Out!

The first of these "narratives" consists in the assertion that Putin annexed Crimea in violation of international law. The truth is, as former Chancellor Helmut Schmidt stressed, that the Ukraine crisis began with the EU Conference in Maastricht [the 1992 conference at which the EU founding treaty was signed] and the subsequent decision by the EU to imperiously expand to the East. The crisis was triggered by the attempt at the EU summit in Vilnius, Lithuania in November 2013, to bring Ukraine under the influence of the EU and NATO through an Association Agreement with the EU.

The bloody Maidan regime-change operation run against Ukraine, was organized by Western-supported NGOs and Bandera Nazis, who were responsible for the Nazi coup in Kiev in February 2014. The developments in Eastern Ukraine and the vote of the people in Crimea (legitimate under international law) to join with Russia were a reaction to that coup. (You can find comprehensive documentation of that process on the BüSo's website.) The truth about the Ukraine crisis must be publicly clarified!

The second narrative—claiming that Russia manipulated the American elections by hacking the DNC's computers—was recently refuted by publication of a memo to President Trump by the Veteran Intelligence Professionals for Sanity (VIPS), and in a tremendously important interview of VIPS member Ray McGovern by LaRouche PAC. Former security specialists, all top experts in their fields, have provided forensic evidence that there was no Russian hacking, but that the data was stolen by insiders and then leaked.

The results of the VIPS investigation must finally become widely known, and their experts invited to hearings in the Bundestag!

A Right Sector torch march in Kiev, Jan. 1, 2014. The group initiated the violence that led to the coup d'état in Ukraine the following month.

Germany, and all the other affected countries, must defend themselves against the extraterritorial claims of the United States that are illegal under international law. The appropriate forum for this would be the UN General Assembly, which convenes in September. It is the obvious body to conduct a hearing on the application of international law in this case.

But the most important step is to establish a totally new and higher level of politics, and of relations among nations. The current course of sanctions, counter-sanctions, trade war, escalation of geopolitical provocations, proxy wars,— where is it supposed to end? In a massive thermonuclear war?

If we Germans have learned anything from the two world wars of the 20th Century, then we should energetically seize the initiative, and not only put the creation of a new Russia policy on the agenda, but take up China's offer for win-win cooperation in building the New Silk Road. Then, together with Russia, China, and other nations, we will rebuild the Near and Middle East, which have been devastated by Blair's, Bush's, and Obama's wars, and we will also develop Africa.

According to polls, 83% of Germans oppose U.S. sanctions against Russia, but 91% are against Trump. It's time that these mass-media-damaged individuals catch on that Trump is not the problem, but in this case, the problem is that the U.S. Congress, with this sanctions vote, is helping to revive the unipolar world order by all available means, even at the cost of the extinction of the human race.

President Trump Refuses To Implement Unconstitutional Congressional Sanctions

In this Aug. 2 statement, President Trump pointed out that the insane sanctions act just passed by the Congress is largely unconstitutional, and served notice that he will not implement its unconstitutional provisions. This is the meaning of the sentence, "My Administration will give careful and respectful consideration to the preferences expressed by the Congress in these various provisions and will implement them in a manner consistent with the President's constitutional authority to conduct foreign relations."

Statement by President Donald J. Trump on the Signing of H.R. 3364:

Today, I have signed into law H.R. 3364, the "Countering America's Adversaries Through Sanctions Act." While I favor tough measures to punish and deter aggressive and destabilizing behavior by Iran, North Korea, and Russia, this legislation is significantly flawed.

In its haste to pass this legislation, the Congress included a number of clearly unconstitutional provisions. For instance, although I share the policy views of sections 253 and 257, those provisions purport to displace the President's exclusive constitutional authority to recognize foreign governments, including their territorial bounds, in conflict with the Supreme Court's recent decision in Zivotofsky v. Kerry.

Additionally, section 216 seeks to grant the Congress the ability to change the law outside the constitutionally required process. The bill prescribes a review period that precludes the President from taking certain actions. Certain provisions in section 216, however, conflict with the Supreme Court's decision in INS v. Chadha, because they purport to allow the Congress to extend the review period through procedures that do not satisfy the requirements for changing the law under Article I, section 7 of the Constitution. I nevertheless expect to honor the bill's extended waiting periods to ensure that the Congress will have a full opportunity to avail itself of the bill's review procedures.

Further, certain provisions, such as sections 254 and 257, purport to direct my subordinates in the executive branch to undertake certain diplomatic initiatives, in contravention of the President's exclusive constitutional authority to determine the time, scope, and objectives of international negotiations. And other provisions, such as sections 104, 107, 222, 224, 227, 228, and 234, would require me to deny certain individuals entry into the United States, without an exception for the President's responsibility to receive ambassadors under Article II, section 3 of the Constitution. My Administration will give careful and respectful consideration to the preferences expressed by the Congress in these various provisions and will implement them in a manner consistent with the President's constitutional authority to conduct foreign relations.

Finally, my Administration particularly expects the Congress to refrain from using this flawed bill to hinder our important work with European allies to resolve the conflict in Ukraine, and from using it to hinder our efforts to address any unintended consequences it may have for American businesses, our friends, or our allies.

DONALD J. TRUMP

Historic Italian-Chinese Agreement on Lake Chad Project

Excerpted from a report in EIR Strategic Alert, *No. 32 of 2017.*

Aug. 7—Backed by their respective governments, the Italian engineering firm Bonifica Spa and PowerChina, one of China's biggest multinationals, have signed a letter of intent for cooperation in exploring the feasibility, and eventually implementing the construction of the largest infrastructure project ever envisioned for Africa—the integrated water-transfer, energy, and transportation infrastructure project called Transaqua.

The letter was signed during a meeting between the executive heads of the two companies in Hangzhou on June 6-8, in the presence of the Italian ambassador to China, but it was only publicly made known at the beginning of August.

Transaqua is an idea developed by Bonifica in the 1970s, to build a 2,400 km-long canal from the southern region of the Democratic Republic of Congo, which would intercept the right-bank tributaries of the Congo River through dams and reservoirs, and carry up to 100 billion cubic meters of water per year, by gravity, to Lake Chad, in order to refill the shrinking lake, and in addition to produce electricity and abundant water for irrigation. The canal would provide a major transportation network for central Africa.

In past decades, the situation around Lake Chad has become more and more explosive and urgent. While the drying-out of the lake has forced a mass emigration to Europe, the impoverishment of the region has become a fertile ground for recruiting terrorists to Boko Haram. Although Transaqua offered a solution to all those problems, Western nations and institutions had so far refused to accept the project, on financial and ideological pretexts.

It is thanks to the fight waged by the LaRouche organization, especially since the late 1970s, together with the authors of the Transaqua idea, that this project can now become reality in the framework of the Belt and Road Initiative. Efforts of the *EIR* and the Schiller Institute created the opportunity for the Lake Chad Basin Commission (LCBC), under Nigerian leadership, and the Transaqua authors to come together. Activity by the *EIR* and the Schiller Institute also led to the

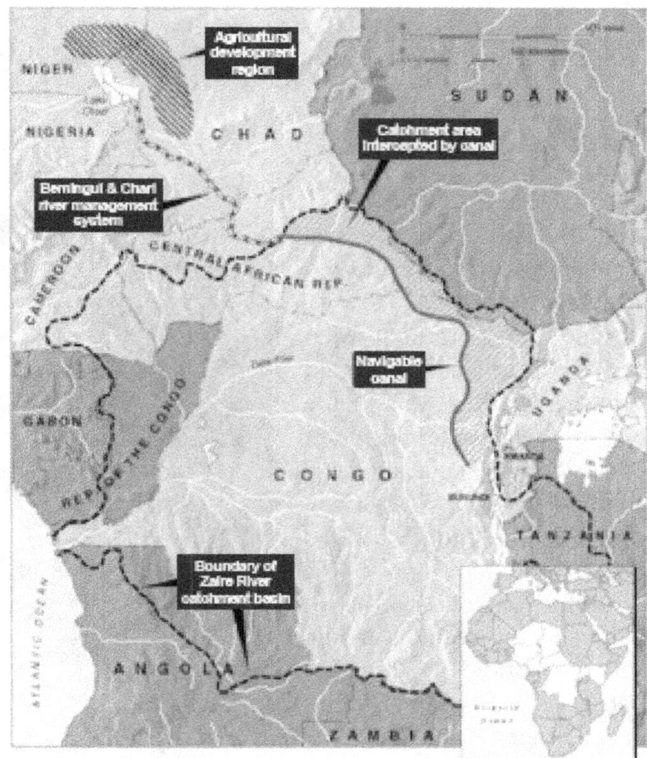

Lake Chad (upper left), Congo (Zaire) River Basin, and proposed projects.

adoption of the view that Transaqua was the only realistic solution for the region. In December 2016, the LCBC signed a Memorandum of Understanding with PowerChina, and eventually organized contact between the Italian and the Chinese companies.

Speaking about the 2016 MOU to the *Nigerian Tribune* July 25, Nigerian Water Minister Suleiman Adamu noted that PowerChina is responsible for the inter-basin transfer. "China is doing exactly the same thing—they are transferring water from southern China to northern China. Just like Nigeria, southern China has more water than the north. In the northern part, some areas are semi-arid, so they are transferring water. The total canal that they built is about 2,500 kilometers, and that is Phase 1."

The head of the LCBC, Engineer Abdullahi Sanusi, expressed his confidence that the new cooperation will succeed "to be part of good history, to bring hope to the voiceless."

Why the Good Samaritan?

by Dean Andromidas

Aug. 4—The July 21 issue of *EIR* was conceptualized around the theme, "How to Rescue our Forgotten Men and Women with Donald Trump." Marking this theme was a remarkable sculpture of the "Good Samaritan" executed by the American sculptor John Quincy Adams Ward.

Astute readers saw the relationship between this theme and the articles within, reporting the political fight being waged to rescue our nation from four decades of economic and cultural degeneration. The economic despair now gripping millions of individuals is most dramatically seen in the reports from New York City, where the precipitous collapse of infrastructure demands the creation of a new productive credit system, the immediate implementation of the Glass-Steagall Act, and an approach to economics and science coherent with Lyndon La-Rouche's *Four Laws*. Nonetheless some our readers, especially younger ones, hoped to see a little more explanation concerning the "forgotten man" and why it was artistically represented with this particular statue.

This article hopefully will fill in the picture.

Wikipedia

The Good Samaritan, by John Quincy Adams Ward, 1867, in Boston Public Gardens.

The Forgotten Man Across the Centuries

In our era, the Twenty-First Century, the recent presidential elections brought to the fore the "forgotten" men and women of our society, left behind by decades of neoliberal policies resting on the greed of a financial oligarchy, in which the fundamental Constitutional theme of the "general welfare" all but disappeared. Yet, "God works in mysterious ways" and gave us a new President, Donald Trump, who in his victory speech last November declared, "The forgotten men and women of our country will be forgotten no longer. Everyone is listening to you now." He then called for national unity, for both Democrats and Republicans to unite and rescue the country from the current crisis.

For the purpose of accuracy, and to further illuminate how change is achieved, it must be added that it was not Donald Trump who was the first to identify the "forgotten man" as the central theme of our time. Lyndon LaRouche declared it the theme of his presidential election campaign in 2000. LaRouche correctly identified that the political stirrings within the American people, as a reaction to the growing injustices of a failing economic and financial policy, would emerge into a movement that would, one way or another, sweep aside the policies of the previous four decades.

It took two disastrous presidential administrations—which together brought forth the Four Horsemen of the Apocalypse: Conquest, War, Famine, and Death—to discredit the policy axioms of the trans-Atlantic establishment, and for the forgotten men and women of this nation to seek a dramatic change. Then, in November of last year, their voices were finally heard.

While the election of Trump has opened the door that had been shut during the era of "Washington consensus," the real struggle has only begun. The nation must now implement the policies to ensure that the "Forgotten men and women of our country will be forgotten no longer. . . ."

The battle before us is intense, and the enemy is desperate.

Franklin Roosevelt's Crusade

The origin of the "forgotten man" as a political theme occurred in the middle of the last century, when it was taken up by Franklin D. Roosevelt, who like Trump, hailed

Roosevelt broadcasts his Fireside Chat on the "forgotten man," April 7, 1932.

from New York City. Roosevelt enunciated his message in a radio address, on April 7, 1932. As everyone knows, that campaign occurred in the middle of the worst economic crisis this nation has ever experienced.

While the entire address can be read, this author wishes to highlight some of the crucial principles identified by Roosevelt.

As Donald Trump was to do, more than eight decades later, FDR calls for national unity in face of the grave crisis endangering the very foundations of the nation. He declares, "I do not want to feel that I am addressing an audience of Democrats or that I speak merely as a Democrat myself. The present condition of our national affairs is too serious to be viewed through partisan eyes for partisan purposes."

FDR then evokes the mobilization during World War I, when, as Assistant Secretary of the Navy, he played an important role:

Fifteen years ago my public duty called me to an

active part in a great national emergency, the World War. Success then was due to a leadership whose vision carried beyond the timorous and futile gesture of sending a tiny army of 150,000 trained soldiers and the regular navy to the aid of our allies. The generalship of that moment conceived of a whole Nation mobilized for war, economic, industrial, social and military resources gathered into a vast unit capable of and actually in the process of throwing into the scales ten million men equipped with physical needs and sustained by the realization that behind them were the united efforts of 110,000,000 human beings. It was a great plan because it was built from bottom to top and not from top to bottom.

Roosevelt adds:

"In my calm judgment, the Nation faces today a

more grave emergency than in 1917," and,

> These unhappy times call for the building of plans that rest upon the forgotten, the unorganized but the indispensable units of economic power, for plans like those of 1917 that build from the bottom up and not from the top down, that put their faith once more in the forgotten man at the bottom of the economic pyramid.

FDR then identifies who the "forgotten man" is and why he suffers. As Lyndon LaRouche has attacked those who call for the magic of "free market reforms," FDR charges, "It is the habit of the unthinking to turn in times like this to the illusions of economic magic." He adds that while expanding government spending on public works to provide emergency employment "would be only a stopgap, a real economic cure must go to the killing of the bacteria in the system rather than to the treatment of external symptoms."

One of those "bacteria" was the fact that the farmers and the agricultural sector of the country, which at that time accounted for almost 50% of the population, were receiving prices for their produce that were less than the cost of production, wiping out the purchasing power of half the country. Thus, while food cartels thought they were making a profit out of "free market" conditions, American industry lost half of its domestic market.

Today, we see the same exploitation in the reality that the forgotten men and women of the Twenty-First Century are being paid wages that do not allow them to support themselves or their families. This destruction of social reproduction deprives the nation of the future generation of skilled workers, scientists, doctors, and others, which constitutes the foundation of any progressing nation.

In his April 7, 1932 address, FDR charges that while the previous Hoover Administration had created a $2 billion fund to bail out the big banks and corporations, that fund did not address the forgotten home-owner and the farm-owner who were being dispossessed in large numbers through foreclosures of their mortgages. Hoover's bailout aided the big banks which were en-

President Franklin Delano Roosevelt talking with a homesteader in North Dakota in 1936.

gaged in speculation, not the little local banks or local loan companies which serviced the local economies. FDR declares, "Here should be an objective of Government itself, to provide at least as much assistance to the little fellow as it is now giving to the large banks and corporations. That is another example of building from the bottom up." One year latter FDR would solve this problem through the Glass-Steagall Act and the National Housing Act.

In the conclusion of his radio address, FDR admonishes the Hoover administration, and he does so in a definitive language, a language which is also precisely apt for describing the outlook and actions of our current neo-liberal establishment over the last sixteen-plus years.

> But they seem to be beyond the concern of a national administration which can think in terms only of the top of the social and economic structure. It has sought temporary relief from the top down rather than permanent relief from the bottom up. It has totally failed to plan ahead in a comprehensive way. It has waited until something has cracked and then at the last moment has sought to prevent total collapse.
>
> It is high time to get back to fundamentals. It is high time to admit with courage that we are in the midst of an emergency at least equal to that of war. Let us mobilize to meet it.

Christ and the Forgotten Man

From a Christian standpoint, Roosevelt's famous address is like a modern parable that parallels the *Good Samaritan* of the **New Testament**. Christ clearly ministers "from the bottom up" among the forgotten men and women to bring "the Kingdom of God on earth as it is in heaven."

The Parable is short enough to quote here:

25. And, behold, a certain lawyer stood up, and tempted him, saying, Master, what shall I do to inherit eternal life?

26. He said unto him, What is written in the law? how readest thou?

27. And he answering said, Thou shalt love the Lord thy God with all thy heart, and with all thy soul, and with all thy strength, and with all thy mind; and thy neighbor as thyself.

28. And he said unto him, Thou hast answered right: this do, and thou shalt live.

29. But he, willing to justify himself, said unto Jesus, And who is my neighbor?

30. And Jesus answering said, A certain man went down from Jerusalem to Jericho, and fell among thieves, which stripped him of his raiment, and wounded him, and departed, leaving him half dead.

31. And by chance there came down a certain priest that way: and when he saw him, he passed by on the other side.

32. And likewise a Levite, when he was at the place, came and looked on him, and passed by on the other side.

33. But a certain Samaritan, as he journeyed, came where he was: and when he saw him, he had compassion on him,

34. And went to him, and bound up his wounds, pouring in oil and wine, and set him on his own beast, and brought him to an inn, and took care of him.

35. And on the morrow when he departed, he took out two pence, and gave them to the host, and said unto him, Take care of him; and whatsoever thou spendest more, when I come again, I will repay thee.

36. Which now of these three, thinkest thou, was neighbor unto him that fell among the thieves?

37. And he said, He that shewed mercy on him. Then said Jesus unto him, Go, and do thou likewise.

Gospel According to Saint Luke, Chapter 10:25-37

The modern parallel is too obvious to dwell on. The naked and beaten traveler is the "forgotten man" and represents the inhuman condition of our society, which currently designates entire classes of people as "useless eaters," or to use Hillary Clinton's language, "deplorables." The "Certain Lawyer" represents those who demand "rule of law" and deny man Justice, the principle upon which all that is worthy of the name "law" rests. The "Priest" is the high priest of the Free Market, who stands for nothing more then cult magic to control the minds and lives of man. The "Levite" is the lackey of that high priest doing the dirty work for his "just" rewards. The Good Samaritan is what we must all become if we are to save our nation and mankind.

Why Express a Universal Principle with a Work of Art?

While the choice of the Good Samaritan as the image for **EIR**'s cover hopefully should be now clear enough, the question remains: why represent it with a work of art? There are many powerful photographic images of the Forgotten Men and Women of yesteryear and today. But such an image would only be half the story; it would only show the suffering without the remedy!

John Quincy Adams Ward's *Good Samaritan* is especially suited to the task. Ward was one of the first true sculptor artists of America. Among his most noted works is George Washington stepping up to take the oath of office of the President, which stands in front of Federal Hall in New York City.[1]

The *Good Samaritan* is part of a larger monument called the Ether Memorial, which commemorates the development of ether as a boon to humanity and medical science. The figures might strike the viewer as rather rough or having strongly accentuated edges: this is because it sits atop a column that is more than thirty feet high. and is viewed from a distance of at least forty or fifty feet. Without the sculptural affectation, the features of the figures would not be discernable.

There are many artistic renderings of the *Good Samaritan*, both as statues and paintings, but few have chosen Ward's particular rendering. Rembrandt exe-

---

1. A fuller background on Ward can be found in the author's "Beautiful City," Part III, *EIR,* July 14, 2017.

cuted a painting depicting the Good Samaritan bringing the traveler to an inn on his donkey. This same scene is executed in stained glass by Ward's good friend and fellow artist, John LaFarge (Trinity Church, Buffalo). Rembrandt also executed many studies of the parable in pen and ink as well as etchings. Nonetheless, the *Good Samaritan* as a sculpture is rare, and examples that do exist are not as successful as Ward's.

The artist chose a very intimate arrangement, where the Good Samaritan cradles the wounded traveler in his arm while ministering to his wounds. Here we have the *evil*: the beaten and robbed traveler, our forgotten man; and the *remedy*, in the image of the Good Samaritan, ministering to his charge. The artist obviously sought to evoke the image of *'Charity,'* as in Paul's *1 Corinthians 13*.

Now Charity is a species of love, different from the love between mother and child, husband and wife, brother and sister. Lyndon LaRouche also defines Charity in a comment on Dante's *Commedia*, where he writes:

> The case of the individual in "Purgatory" helps to instruct us, that to realize the high self-interest in the Good, it is not sufficient to be able to recognize the good descriptively, or even to be inspired by the desire to achieve what he describes as Good. We must become Good; we must be governed in impulses respecting our immediately personal self interest by the good. That Good must become our immediate self-interest, our immediate motivation in every aspect of personal life. To achieve that congruence of personal, self-interested impulses and service of the Good, is the condition of "Paradise."...

This presents the greatest challenge to the artist and most particularly the sculptor, who must evoke an intellectual and emotional response from the viewer through the hard, cold medium of stone. For him,

The Good Samaritan, by Rembrandt van Rijn, 1633.

Charity must be also an artistic principle; without it his work is "as the sounding brass, or tinkling of cymbal." It is this principle of Charity that breaths life into stone.

There is no formula to achieve this; yet, we see it clearly in Ward's rendering of the face of the Good Samaritan, and also, incredibly, in his hands, one carefully but firmly cradling the traveler's shoulder and the other ever so carefully, even delicately, ministering to the wounds as to avoid inflicting more pain on his charge. The sculpture indeed depicts the "self-interested impulses and service of the Good...".

Thus, *EIR* has marshaled Ward's work of art into an effort to mobilize citizens not simply to do good deeds, but to make society good through joining in our political efforts.

The American System Must Prevail: Implement LaRouche's Four Laws Now!

by Kesha Rogers

Two systems are before the world ... one looks to pauperism, ignorance, depopulation and barbarism; the other to increasing wealth, comfort, intelligence, combination of action, and civilization. One looks toward universal war; the other to universal peace. One is the English system, the other we may be proud to call the American system; for it is the only one ever devised the tendency of which was that of elevating while equalizing the conditions of man throughout the world.

—Henry Carey,
The Harmony of Interests, 1851

Aug. 4—The above words were composed one hundred and sixty-six years ago. It is a damning charge against the follies of our recent political leadership that, today, we find ourselves at a strategic fork in the road, where once again there are "two systems before the world," two alternative paths, and it is the "path taken" which will determine the future for all of humanity. One is the pathway of global economic development, prosperity, and peace. This is the system of China's Belt and Road Initiative, epitomized in its "win win" philosophy. That philosophy, and the magnificent economic development projects now under construction, are fully and beauti-

National Archives

Re-enact Glass-Steagall: *Franklin D, Roosevelt signs Glass-Steagall Act, 1933.*

CC/Davidt8

National Banking: *Hamilton's First Bank of the United States (1797-1811).*

wikipedia

Infrastructure: *Norris Dam constructed by FDR's Tennessee Valley Authority.*

PPPL

Fusion-Driver Program: *National Spherical Torus Experiment (NSTX) facility.*

fully coherent with Carey's imperative for "elevating while equalizing the conditions of man throughout the world." The second pathway is the monetarist system of looting. This is the system of the dying trans-Atlantic imperial financial system, a now bankrupt monetary house of cards that has only managed to stave off annihilation over the recent decades through a combination of unbridled financial speculation, war, and brutal austerity against the people of the United States and countless others in Europe and most of the rest of the world.

As Lyndon LaRouche declared strongly this week, "We have to cancel the British system. This is what is destroying the income and function of the people of the United States. They should declare a freedom from the British system." Lyndon LaRouche's Four Laws represent a clear pathway out of the escalating global financial crisis and danger of thermonuclear war between the USA and Russia. Bringing an urgently needed program of industrial and physical economic growth to save the American people from mass suicide, drug overdose, and fear of the future, means once and for all taking away the power of Wall Street to decide the fate of humanity. This will require immediately accepting China's offer to cooperate in the global Belt and Road Initiative. This quality of paradigm shift is key to humanity launching a new era and to advancing an industrial and scientific breakthrough in the United States that generates a higher quality of life,—to free people so they may again look to a future of hope and optimism for a better world, and of promoting growth, and "win-win" cooperation, around the world.

LaRouche's Four Laws

Three years ago, Lyndon LaRouche authored "The Four New Laws to Save the U.S.A. Now!" LaRouche identified four key areas that must become the basis for policy in order to save our United States from destruction. The efforts of *EIR* and LaRouche PAC have been unceasing and relentless over the last thirty-eight months in fighting for LaRouche's solution to the current crisis. Yet it is clear that the overwhelming majority of elected officials, particularly in Congress, have either ignored LaRouche's expertise or been unwilling to act in the necessary way. It is time for the American people to force these measures through the Congress and the Presidency. The American people must go on the offensive and move now, to abolish the Wall Street casino economy and its war machine, now, and bring forth a new paradigm of optimism and growth for mankind.

In summary, LaRouche's Four Laws are:

1. The immediate re-enactment of the Glass-Steagall law, instituted by U.S. President Franklin D. Roosevelt, without modification, as to principle of action.

2. A return to a system of top-down and thoroughly defined National Banking.

3. The deployment of a Federal Credit system, to generate high-productivity trends in improvements of employment, to increase the physical-economic productivity and the standard of living of the persons and households of the United States.

4. Adopt a Fusion-Driver "Crash Program." The essential distinction of man from all lower forms of life, in practice, is that it presents the means for the perfection of the specifically affirmative aims and needs of human individual and social life.

Let Hamilton Guide Us

True economic value, as defined by Alexander Hamilton, starts with the promotion of the creative powers of the human mind. It advances a pro-human, pro-science, and pro-growth culture, as opposed to the British system of fake economic value that starts with the promotion of monetary profit and the bestialization of the human mind. The British system advances an anti-human, anti-science, and pro-death culture. The acceptance of the British system in America has resulted in permanent Wall Street bailouts, wars, civil strife, drug addiction, mass hysteria in popular opinions, and a total lack of vision for the future.

The year 2017 marks the one hundredth birthday of two great visionaries, President John Kennedy and space pioneer Krafft Ehricke. Together, their dedication and inspiration decades ago created a new wave of optimism, inspiring the imagination of the next generation of explorers as never seen before. That is why today we can celebrate the forty-eighth anniversary of the first Apollo Moon landing. This great achievement, which propelled mankind into a new era on July 20, 1969, did not happen as a result of random chance. It was a result of hard work, dedication to a better world, and setting a future mission for the progress of mankind in our Solar system and beyond.

President Kennedy understood that exploration of space and shared breakthroughs in scientific discoveries were instrumental to future cooperation among nations, ending the threat of war, eradicating disease and ending poverty. Kennedy declared in his first inaugural address, "Let both sides seek to invoke the wonders of science instead of its terrors. Together let us explore the stars, conquer the deserts, eradicate disease, tap the ocean depths and encourage the arts and commerce." President Kennedy went on to say, "All this will not be finished in the first one hundred days. Nor will it be finished in the first one thousand days, nor in the life of this Administration, nor even perhaps in our lifetime on this planet. But let us begin."

So did President Kennedy begin, as he called on a new generation of leaders to join him in the new beginning, of ensuring economic growth and progress throughout the nation. Young people from all over signed up to take part in this great mission that had been set by the President to be fulfilled before the end of the decade. Much was done in subsequent years to set the course of progress back and to prevent the nation from realizing the vision of President Kennedy. The President's murder was followed by the launching of the anti-growth environmental agenda, and massive budget cuts. Engineers, astronauts, and space pioneers faced many challenges, but they were determined, despite the many obstacles and setbacks. Failure was not an option.

Voters elected Donald Trump for an end to perpetual war, and for Glass-Steagall. President Trump speaks during a rally in Nashville, Tennessee on March 15, 2017.

youtube

Today, Let Us Choose the Right Path

The same British empire that opposed Kennedy continues to attempt to brutally enforce its system of usury, universal war, and depopulation on the people of the world. This, at the very time that the world is being led into a new paradigm by Russia and China, who refuse to allow the true cause of the American System to be tossed into the waste bin while mankind is destroyed by total war and annihilation. *Russia and China are not our enemy*; Wall Street, as the tool of the British empire, is. We can break the back of the British empire once and for all by reversing the effects of the coup that killed President John F. Kennedy. Today, that same coup is being run against a legitimately elected President Donald Trump, by those who have orchestrated the fabricated lie of "Russian hacking" into the United States' election process. They have generated the lie to destroy the Presidency of Donald Trump, and to keep the United States in a state of perpetual war and economic disintegration. President Trump can defeat this coup. The lie has been exposed. [See the VIPS memo.]

Let us return to the economic system of the specific intent of the original U.S. Constitution, as defined by our first Treasury Secretary, Alexander Hamilton.[1] Let us use the economic methods he established at our nation's foundation to achieve what Henry Carey later wrote about, by realizing the vision for humanity of Krafft Ehricke and President John Kennedy, with Lyndon LaRouche's scientifically precise guidance at this current conjunctural crisis.

Let us reject the "fake news" that money has some intrinsic value, independent of what it does. The new national credit that must be issued through a Glass-Steagall protected national banking system—to rebuild our nation's infrastructure, industries, and farms, and advance to the era of fusion power—requires us to understand that Credit is a means to an end, rather than an end in and of itself. We advance a national credit program, as Lyndon LaRouche calls for in his four economic laws, "to generate high productivity trends in improvement of employment, with the intention to increase the physical-economic productivity and standard of living of the persons and households of the United States," rather than just to "get rich." Hamilton's notion of real economic value requires the promotion of the creative powers of the human mind. It requires a pro-human, pro-science, and pro-growth culture.

Implement LaRouche's Four Laws now. Let us bring the United States into the New Silk Road to benefit all. Let us restore our commitment to universal peace, through realizing mankind's common mission and common destiny in the universe. Let us explore and develop the Solar system and the vastness beyond, together, restoring our mission and vision for our nation, and for the world.

---

1. See Hamilton's Four Reports to Congress.

Tillerson Charts a Course Toward a New Era of International Collaboration for Peaceful Growth

by Stanley Ezrol

Aug. 6—Secretary of State Rex Tillerson met with journalists at the State Department Aug. 1, to update and clarify the nature of the Trump Administration's foreign policy. This discussion came at a time when most news media in the United States were presenting an image of an administration wracked with chaotic internal conflicts, while being aggressively investigated for illegal collusion with Russia and China in opposition to the interests of the United States.

These reports would have one think that top personnel in the administration were constantly at odds with each other, with the aspirations of the American people, and with the interests of the United States. In this situation, Secretary Tillerson presented a sweeping discussion of current policy, policy which could create great new possibilities in world affairs over the next fifty years, in the context of reviewing the major historic developments of the last fifty.

Although a complete transcript of his remarks and a video are available through the State Department, most news media chose to cover mere scraps of Tillerson's remarks, to contribute to the notion that U.S. foreign policy is hopelessly confused. Tillerson acknowledged that we are confronted with grave difficulties, but his remarks, together with the decisive signing statements President Trump issued the next day rejecting the attempt by Congress to destroy our positive relations with China and Russia with unconstitutional sanctions, ought to make it clear that we now have a Secretary of State and a Presidency with a mature commitment to a strategy of global cooperation such as we have not seen in decades.

Xinhua/Bao Dandan

U.S. State Secretary Rex Tillerson delivers a speech to State Department employees in Washington, D.C., May 3, 2017.

Tillerson began by emphasizing that the Trump Administration is unalterably committed to "Making America Great Again," but emphasized that when President Trump says, "America first," he does not mean "America alone." He explained that despite difficulties, disagreements, and potential conflicts, the administration is committed to mutually beneficial collaboration on areas of agreement, and avoidance of open conflict over situations where collaboration is not achievable. Much of his presentation explained how the administration is approaching each major area of tension in the world on that basis.

He added that looking back 50 years, there was a major change at the end of the cold war, and that major changes—most notably what he called a "pivot point" due to the dramatic expansion of China's role in the world—continue to occur. In these areas of change

Tillerson noted that President Trump has challenged many of the policies he's inherited. Tillerson gave assurances that the administration is not necessarily "throwing these things away," but asking, "How should we define these relationships to serve the American people's interest, obviously, first and foremost? But in doing so, I think we're confident it serves the global interest and the interest of our partners and allies as well."

North Korea

Tillerson elaborated that the development of administration policy toward North Korea starts with a campaign of "peaceful pressure" to avoid other options that he described as "not particularly attractive." He indicated that the administration hoped that this approach would "develop a willingness [for North Korea] to sit and talk with us and others, but with an understanding that a condition of those talks is that there is no future where North Korea holds nuclear weapons or the ability to deliver those nuclear weapons to anyone in the region, much less to the homeland." The administration engaged China in this effort because "we share the same objective, a denuclearized Korean Peninsula" and because China, which accounts for 90% of North Korea's international trade "can put pressure on and influence the North Korean regime in ways that no one else can." Perhaps to answer China's objection that North Korea's quarrel is primarily with the United States, and that U.S. actions cannot be effective without changes in the relations of the United States with North Korea—particularly in light of the history of the U.S. assault against Iraq and Libya—Tillerson explained that in our relations with North Korea "we do not seek a regime change; we do not seek the collapse of the regime; we do not seek an accelerated reunification of the peninsula; we do not seek an excuse to send our military north of the 38th parallel. And we're trying to convey to the North Koreans we are not your enemy, we are not your threat, but you are presenting an unacceptable threat to us, and we have to respond."

Xinhua

U.S. Secretary of State Rex Tillerson (right) and Secretary of Defense James Mattis give a press briefing after the U.S.-China Diplomatic and Security Dialogue in Washington, D.C., June 21, 2017.

China

After addressing the North Korea crisis, Tillerson turned to the issue of China, explaining "I think it's important that everyone understand that North Korea does not define the relationship with China." He recounted the opening up of U.S./China relationships fifty years ago, during the Nixon Administration, and the commitment to collaboration established at the Mar-a-Lago summit between Presidents Trump and Xi Jinping. He then referred to the "pivot point" defined by the fact that China is now the second largest economy in the world, "and they will continue to grow in their importance to the global economy," then asking, "What should define this relationship for the next 50 years?" This, he said, should be based on ensuring "economic prosperity to the benefit of both countries and the world," and that inevitable differences are resolved "in a way that does not lead to open conflict."

Then he referred to the disputes over the South China Sea, which the U.S. media and others have painted as a major threat to the peace and security of the United States and the nations in the area, remarking simply, "And where we have differences—in the South China Sea, and we have some trading differences that need to be addressed—can we work through those differences in a way without it leading to open conflict, and find the solutions that are necessary to serve us both?"

He pointed to the four high-level dialogues established at Mar-a-Lago. The first, the Diplomatic and Security Dialogue led by Tillerson, Secretary of Defense James Mattis, and their Chinese counterparts, has met twice. The Economic and Trade Dialogue, led on the U.S. side by Secretary of Commerce Wilbur Ross and Treasury Secretary Steve Mnuchin, has also met twice. The Law Enforcement and Cyber Security Dialogue and the People-to-People Dialogue have not yet met.

This approach to China, as well as the approach to Russia described below, is directly opposite to the geopolitical expressions of President Obama, Hillary Clinton, the neo-cons regardless of party affiliation, and the Democratic Party Congressional leadership today. The hideously evil view of that latter crew is that nuclear war must be at least risked, if not waged, to destroy any power that has achieved a status that might threaten the world domination of Britain and its allies, not because of anything they have done or threatened to do, but simply because of their ability to threaten the empire. This, incidentally, explains why the Cold War that many people naively believe was a conflict between communism and capitalism, is being revived almost thirty years after the collapse of European communism. The public founder of the Cold War, Winston Churchill, and his allies, have made it clear repeatedly, that their cause was neither capitalism nor freedom, but the destruction of threats to the existence of the empire.

Russia

Next Tillerson turned to the relationship with Russia. He recalled that on his first trip to Moscow to meet with President Vladimir Putin, Putin had said "the relationship was at a historic low since the end of the Cold War and it could get worse." Tillerson then asked, "Is it getting worse, or can we maintain some level of stability in that relationship, and continue to find ways to address areas of mutual interest and ways in which we can deal with our differences without those becoming open conflicts as well?"

Tillerson discussed the working relationship in the war against ISIS in Syria, saying both powers are committed to the defeat of ISIS and the other terrorist organizations, and both are committed to a unified Syria in which the Syrian people arrange a new constitution, in which the threat of post-ISIS civil war is averted, and they conduct free and fair elections to choose their leadership. The United States and Russia disagree on the future of the elected President, Bashar al-Assad. He noted that Russia has aligned itself with Assad, but that the United States finds him unacceptable. In fact, President Putin and his government have said that they are now cooperating with the elected president, but that the future leadership of Syria is up to the Syrian people. Despite these differences, a zone of "deconfliction" has been achieved and is holding steady, and the United States and Russia are collaborating in expanding this to other regions of Syria. As for the differences with Russia, Tillerson said, "The sequencing of all that we're open to, as long as that is what is achieved at the end."

Thus, although Tillerson has explained U.S. differences with Russia, the Administration is not letting these hold up the peace process. He does not mention the potential conflict between the goal of eventually ousting Assad, and that of permitting the Syrians to choose their own government. He also does not mention the fact, often raised by the governments of Syria and Russia, that Russia is legitimately providing military aid to the internationally recognized government of Syria, whereas the United States, while cooperating to some extent with Russia and the Assad government, is not a legitimate guest of Syria. Despite the U.S. misgivings about Assad, President Trump has withdrawn support for militias that have been fighting against his government. Clearly, the Trump Administration is leaving room for further reconciliation with Russia in this area.

The other area of tension with Russia that Tillerson mentioned is Ukraine. He insisted that the Minsk accords must be implemented, but Russia agrees with this. They do disagree on the interpretation of Minsk. He pointed to the appointment of special representative Kurt Volker, which Russia has welcomed, to move the reconciliation process further.

The Middle East and ISIS

Tillerson then outlined the progress being made against ISIS in Iraq, stating that approximately two million Iraqis have been able to return home. He emphasized that the U.S. role in this is to secure areas in cooperation with local law enforcement, to help local leaders return to their communities, and restore basic needs like power, water, and sewage. "That's where we stop," he said, "We're not there to rebuild their communities. That's for them to do and that's for the international community."

He referenced the "grand coalition" of 68 countries

U.S. Secretary of State Rex Tillerson (right), with U.S. Secretary of Homeland Security John Kelly, at a press conference in Mexico City, Feb. 23, 2017.

the United States has worked with, and stated that the intention is to recognize ISIS as a global threat that has now surfaced in the Philippines and threatens Southeast Asia. He also referred to the need to battle terrorism in cyberspace, a recruiting arena for ISIS.

Tillerson mentioned the successful agreement with Iran to curtail its nuclear weapons program, but asserted that it is conducting other destabilizing activities and is attempting to expand into Yemen, Iraq, Syria, and Afghanistan. This approach is one that Russia openly disagrees with. Tillerson also failed to address the dire humanitarian disaster, including a massive cholera epidemic and widespread famine, in Yemen, caused by Saudi Arabia's U.S.-backed war against its tiny neighbor. Nonetheless, the Administration has not cut off contact with the concerned parties.

Western Hemisphere

Tillerson reported on his trip with then Secretary of Homeland Security John Kelly, to establish cooperation with Mexico. They established a "framework" to attack the drug cartels and other criminal organizations. A large part of U.S. responsibility in this, he said, is that "we are the customer," and he said that the Department of Health and Human Services will be working on attacking that problem at home. He reported a 70% to 80% reduction in illegal border crossings.

Other concerns expressed in this hemisphere include working on security and prosperity for Central America, and the reduction of violence and return to democracy in Venezuela.

The State Department

Secretary Tillerson has come under attack in the media and by some foreign policy experts, including unnamed State Department officials, for operating independently of the foreign policy professionals. He addressed this throughout his talk by commending by name the career diplomats who made positive contributions to every initiative he discussed. In addressing the organizational problem directly, he pointed out that only one of the six under-secretary positions in the department has been filled. In the State Department, under secretaries rank just below the deputy secretary, and they direct the major branches of the Department, so this is a critical shortcoming. He also reported that many of the assistant secretary positions that rank just below the under secretaries, are filled with "acting" officers. Nonetheless, Tillerson said, the professional foreign service officers have made it possible for the department to accomplish what it has in his first six months in office. He added that he meets with his staff on the Under Secretary and Assistant Secretary level several times a week, and is in touch with staff at all levels, through lunches and other means. In responding to a question on this, he said that he expected, given the radical change in administration, that some would have difficulty in making the transition, but that most had committed themselves. For those who objected to a particular responsibility, he offered them the option of switching to something they would do willingly, rather than having people in place who objected to their assignments.

Tillerson reported on his handling of a redesign of the State Department. Based on his experience in private business management, he is leading an "employee-led effort" that began with a survey soliciting input from all employees.

The Administration

The first question asked of Tillerson involved the misunderstandings created by President Trump's tweets

President Trump's first cabinet meeting. He is flanked by Secretary of State Tillerson (left) and Secretary of Defense James Mattis (right).

and the appointment of John Kelly as White House Chief of staff. Rather than choosing to refer this question, as "professional" Secretaries of State and their spokespeople would do, to the White House, Tillerson answered directly. He said that based on his collaboration with Kelly on the issues in Mexico, he thinks he will do a fine job, and that President Trump would not have appointed him if he did not want real change at the White House. He frankly explained his attitude to the President's tweets as well, saying, "It's part of the environment in which we work. We'll adapt to it. There's a lot of unexpected things that happen to us in the world of diplomacy and we know how to adapt to that, so I don't view it as an obstacle, a hindrance, or as an assistance. Whatever the President chooses to express, he expresses, and then that's information to everybody, us included."

The last question to him involved Secretary Tillerson's relationship to the President. His answer was unusually frank for an on-the-record press conference. He said his relationship with Trump is good. "The President has repeatedly expressed his confidence in me; I talk to him just about every day. I see him several times a week. He calls me late at night on the weekends when something comes into his head and he wants to talk. He may call me at any moment at any time, but it is a very open relationship, and it's one in which I feel quite comfortable telling him my views. And he and I have differences of views on things like JCPOA [the nuclear treaty with Iran] and how we should use it. I think if we're not having those differences, I'm not sure I'm serving him. The relationship between the President and myself is good. That's how I view it anyway."

The Future Is Ours To Win or Lose

Tillerson's remarks make it clear that this administration has acted with a higher level of wisdom and responsibility than any in recent memory. It also, as Trump's signing statements demonstrate, has not lost the will or the ability to surprise its enemies with effective countermeasures. They have expressed laudable goals including improving our productive capabilities, making affordable health care available, and putting Americans back to work. The expressed intention to collaborate with the Chinese Belt and Road Initiative is also a tremendous improvement over the previous administration's animosity against Chinese growth. Despite these intentions, and President Trump's references to the American System of economics, and to the restoration of Franklin Roosevelt's Glass-Steagall Act, the Administration has not demonstrated a clear understanding that the whole institution of money as it has been used up until now has to be scrapped, and replaced with a system in which the requirements of the future dictate what economic developments take place and are allocated financial resources accordingly.

In the area of foreign policy *per se*, the administration has rejected the poison of geopolitics as the basis for policy. Unfortunately, as in the approach to South Korea, Iran, Russia, and China, it has not totally put the deadly legacy of Obama Administration policies behind us.

The Trump Administration has done far more than we had a right to hope for, because of our own neglect of our nation's policies. Now it is up to every American to recognize that it is their own ability to rise above the geopolitical lunacies perpetrated by the failed Wall Street "establishment"—and get under the skin of their compatriots to build a tidal wave for the New Silk Road policies designed by Lyndon and Helga LaRouche and adopted by China, Russia, and other governments representing the majority of the world's population—that will carry us past the danger of economic collapse or nuclear conflict to a future in which the fight for creative development is our only conflict.

A Case Study of the British Coup Against the U.S. Presidency

by Barbara Boyd

Aug. 7—This report covers events which occurred in June of 2016, shortly after Donald Trump secured the Republican nomination for President against every wing of the establishment Republican Party, from so-called Tea Party conservatives like Ted Cruz, to Jeb Bush, once thought a shoo-in to become the President of the United States. It aims to show you the British hand in concocting the *coup d'etat* presently underway against the President of the United States. It does so by taking you through British

The "Russian election meddling" hoax begins. Here, CNN asks Prof. Stephen Cohen for his opinion.

intelligence's role in the "Russia meddled in the U.S. election" hoax, and the Trump Tower meeting on June 9, 2016. This meeting, which the media keeps hyping as a "smoking gun," demonstrating Trump campaign "collusion with the Russians," has also drawn major attention from Special Prosecutor Robert Mueller, according to news reports. It has also been the subject of recent hearings and investigations by the Senate Judiciary Committee and Senate Intelligence Committee.

We will not deal here with every aspect of the British role in the ongoing coup. Rather, we are only going to focus on one month, June 2016, to demonstrate the incredible density of British operations aimed at swinging the election toward Hillary Clinton and the geopolitical forces at work in this operation.

The ongoing coup against Trump has exposed very dirty Anglo-American geopolitical operations and the personages behind them, which were never intended for public view. That is the case with the events here.

The Anglo-American elites are desperate and therefore reckless. The trans-Atlantic Ponzi scheme which is their financial empire teeters on the verge of collapse, and with it, any remaining popular respect for their power or competence. They view China and Russia as rising world powers which will dominate the world based on superior economic programs, resources, popular morale, and scientific competence. They have no answer within their dying system. Rather than joining in a new economic platform which could truly advance humanity, as Lyndon and Helga LaRouche have proposed—an idea now flourishing in China's "One Belt-One Road" project—they choose to preserve the dominance of their power at any cost, and are propelling us, rapidly now, to a war which could end the human race.

Most Americans are deeply disturbed by the ongoing coup against the President and don't believe that the accusations being made against him are true. But,

Senator John McCain (left) at a hearing on cybersecurity.

Senator Chuck Schumer.

they are ignorant of their British origins and intent. The British empire, that oligarchical grouping which controls the world's economy through the machinations of the City of London, Wall Street, and related soft- and hard-power institutions, is fighting for its survival against the potential represented by Donald Trump. This empire is the occupying power which has destroyed the United States by the same methods it used to shock Russia into full-scale economic collapse and chaos in the 1990s, resulting in an overt genocide against the Russian population. If you don't know about this genocide and its causes, you really can't understand their demonization of Putin, who has restored the Russian state.

In a rational world, the key figures in the coup against the President would be engulfed in investigations by the Justice Department and Congress, and well on their way to prison. It is, after all, the British and their U.S. pawns, on Wall Street and in Washington—not the Russians—who have looted our country for decades and are now seeking to change the election result. But we do not live in a rational world presently. Rather, we now stand on the verge of an insane nuclear war. Since many in Congress and executive intelligence agencies are active participants in the coup, it is now up to our nation's citizens to rapidly educate themselves in order to procure safe passage for humanity into the next 50 years. They must ensure that any politician who stands in the way no longer holds elective office.

Dramatis Personae

The target audience for *EIR* is the *informed reader*. Nevertheless, given the density of British operations into which we now sail, and in order to "keep the players straight," we provide this abbreviated cast of characters:

Persons of Interest

- **Christopher Steele**—the "former" British MI6 (the foreign intelligence agency of the British government) desk chief for Russia. The founder of Orbis Business Intelligence, Ltd., itself deeply connected to the highest levels Britain's intelligence and financial elite. The author of the December 2016, "dodgy dossier," which alleges massive Russian penetration of, and influence over, the Trump presidential campaign.
- **Dmitri Alperovitch**—the co-founder and chief technology officer of CrowdStrike. A Ukrainian-American who demonizes Putin, and a fellow at the Atlantic Council's Digital Forensics Project, which itself operates within NATO's British-inspired Strategic Communications Service. This organization employs propaganda for war and has targeted Russian President Vladimir Putin.
- **William (Bill) Browder**—a former associate of both British billionaire Robert Maxwell and international money launderer Edmond Safra, Browder made a fortune in the post-1989 asset-stripping and looting of Russia. Banned from Russia in 2005 as a threat to state security. It was the arrest and death of Browder's accountant Sergei Magnitsky, which led to the anti-Russian Magnitsky Act sanctions. Browder, together with Safra, was the founder of Hermitage Capital Management in 1996, a private investment fund based in the unregulated tax havens of Guernsey and

In the photo, MI6, Britain's foreign intelligence agency.

the Cayman Islands. Browder currently operates with the international dope money laundering bank, HSBC.

- **Various Congressional servants of the British, including sitting Senators John McCain, Ben Cardin, Chuck Schumer, and those, like David Kramer**, long associated, with **"Project Democracy,"** a joint U.S.-British operation which has engaged in coups and regime change operations throughout the world, including in Ukraine. Kramer was Assistant Secretary of State for Democracy, Human Rights, and Labor (2008-9), and president of Freedom House (2010-2014).

Institutions and Events of Interest

- **Orbis**—a London-based "private intelligence firm," founded in 2009, Orbis is connected to the highest levels of British intelligence and the circles of former Prime Minister Tony Blair. Supporters of Hillary Clinton "paid" Orbis well over a million dollars to produce dirt on Trump's Russia connections.
- **Fusion GPS**—a strategic intelligence firm based in Washington, D.C., founded in 2009.
- **CrowdStrike**—a private American cybersecurity company, co-founded by Dmitri Alperovitch, which was hired by the Democratic National Committee (DNC), and was responsible for the initial claim that the Russians had "hacked" the DNC servers.
- **GCHQ** (the Government Communications Headquarters)—essentially Britain's equivalent of the National Security Agency.
- **Magnitsky Act**—a 2012 Act designed to "punish" Russian officials for the death of Sergei Magnitsky in a Moscow prison in 2009. Sponsored by Senators

John McCain, Ben Cardin, and Joe Lieberman after a major lobbying campaign by very highly placed, Washington lobbyists.

The Cardinal June Events

Some time in **June 2016**, Hillary Clinton's campaign took over an opposition research project on Donald Trump, which had previously been funded by Trump's Republican opponents. The contract was with a Washington, D.C. firm called *Fusion GPS*, which, in turn, employed a British firm, Orbis Business Intelligence, Ltd., and Orbis' founder Christopher Steele. Orbis was tasked with smearing Donald Trump as a "Manchurian candidate," a pawn of Russian intelligence. Steele and Orbis had maintained a long relationship, dating from 2010, with the FBI. The Clinton campaign has admitted that it was already working with Ukrainian intelligence to tar Trump with the "Russian" brush prior to the June 2016 contract with British intelligence and Orbis.

On **June 12, 2016**, Julian Assange of WikiLeaks announced that he was in possession of emails damaging to Hillary Clinton and would soon be publishing them. The purloined DNC emails showed, definitively, that the DNC, supposed to be neutral in the primary, was trying to destroy the rising campaign of fellow Democrat Bernie Sanders.[1] Two days later, on June 14, the DNC announced that its computers had been hacked by

---

1. The emails were subsequently published by WikiLeaks on the eve of the Democratic National Convention.

Jared Kushner (left) with Trump, at victory party after the Iowa caucuses.

the Russians. The claim that the WikiLeaks emails were the result of a Russian hack of DNC servers was authored by Dmitri Alperovitch of CrowdStrike. Alperovitch, as we shall see, is also deeply connected to NATO.

Three days earlier, on **June 9, 2016**, a meeting took place in Trump Tower involving Donald Trump, Jr., Paul Manafort (the then-campaign manager for the Trump Presidential campaign), Jared Kushner, the President's son-in-law, and five other people. Contrary to media accounts, only one of the participants in the Trump Tower meeting was a Russian, the lawyer Natalia Veselnitskaya. By all accounts provided by participants, the meeting was very short, and involved the Magnitsky Act sanctions imposed by the U.S. Congress on certain Russians. Many consider these 2012 sanctions to be the opening shot of the New Cold War. But the emails setting up the meeting bear all the marks of an intelligence agency entrapment attempt against Donald Trump, Jr., designed to seal the "Manchurian candidate" label early on in the general election campaign. They specifically offered "dirt" on Hillary Clinton to be provided by the Russian government itself.

On July 15, 2016, at the same time that the FBI was opening an investigation of the Russians for interfering in the U.S. election and the Trump campaign for colluding with them, Bill Browder was filing a complaint with the U.S. Department of Justice, concerning four participants in the Trump Tower meeting—and others—for failure to register under the Foreign Agents Registration Act. Browder's complaint claimed that these people were engaged in unregistered Russian lobbying activities, namely, attempting to overturn the Magnitsky Act. As we shall show, much evidence points to Browder being a deep penetration agent for British intelligence and financial interests, who thoroughly snookered the U.S. Congress, and others, with his Magnitsky Act tale. Browder's recent appearance before the Senate Judiciary Committee on July 27, 2017, concerning the Trump Tower meeting and related events, played a big role in the public relations campaign resulting in imposition of new sanctions against Russia. These sanctions are aimed at preventing the President from establishing decent relations with the world's only other nuclear superpower, and they have been described as a declaration of economic war against Russia.

The Very British Roots of This Entire Affair

It is, of course, by now widely acknowledged that the British dodgy dossier on Trump, authored by Christopher Steele and Orbis, formed the initial backbone of the FBI's investigation of the Trump campaign "officially" opened in July 2016, according to the testimony of former FBI Director James Comey. According to its leaks to the *Guardian* and other British newspapers, British intelligence had been loudly complaining about Trump's "softness" on Russia to their American intelligence counterparts since 2015, demanding action, and the British spy agency, GCHQ, which monitors the entire world's Internet and telephone traffic had been tasked to target the American presidential political campaign, based on this "concern."

A May 18, 2017 court filing in the High Court of Justice in Britain by Christopher Steele and Orbis, fills out important aspects of the operation. The filing oc-

These Reports Allege Trump Has Deep Ties To Russia

A dossier, compiled by a person who has claimed to be a former British intelligence official, alleges Russia has compromising information on Trump. The allegations are unverified, and the report contains errors.

A dossier making explosive — but unverified — allegations that the Russian government has been "cultivating, supporting and assisting" President-elect Donald Trump for years and gained compromising information about him has been circulating among elected officials, intelligence agents, and journalists for weeks.

The dossier, which is a collection of memos written over a period of months, includes specific,

A sample from the mass media's pervasive campaign of fabrications against Trump.

curred in the defamation suit brought against Steele and Orbis by Aleksej Gubarev[2] and his companies, who were falsely accused of criminal activities in Steele's now infamous December 2016 dodgy dossier against Trump. It was this salacious and disgusting dossier which Comey used when Obama's intelligence chiefs met with Trump in January 2017, in order to blackmail the President to abandon any idea of accommodation with Putin or Russia. When Trump didn't budge, Steele's dossier was published by *Buzzfeed*, with a stamp of approval from the intelligence chiefs.

According to the court filing, Fusion GPS and Orbis have a confidentiality agreement governing an ongoing business relationship dating back to 2010. The media account up to this point has been that Fusion GPS, hired by Trump's GOP primary opponents to produce dirt on Trump, reached out to Steele and his companies in June 2016, when Fusion's "oppo" work was taken over by Hillary Clinton's donors. In case anyone doubts the deep British intelligence ties at issue here: Steele ran the Russia desk for Britain's MI6 until 2009, and Sir Andrew Wood, an "associate" at Steele's company, was the British Ambassador to Moscow between 1995 and 2000. Wood is also an associate fellow of the Russia and Eurasia Program at the Royal Institute of International Affairs at Chatham House in London, and served as Russia adviser to Prime Minister Tony Blair. Christopher Burrows, Steele's partner in Orbis, lists himself as a long-time high ranking British foreign service officer, although news accounts also place him in British intelligence.

Christopher Steele has also acknowledged a long-standing relationship to the FBI, centered in the FBI's Eurasian Organized Crime Strike Force in New York City, which media reports date to 2010, the same time the relationship with Fusion GPS went into effect. Steele acknowledges playing a major role in the years-long FBI investigation of the International Federation of Association Football (FIFA).[3] He continued to work with the FBI's Eurasian Organized Crime Strike Force on Russian and Ukrainian matters from 2013 to 2016, according to press accounts. Andrew McCabe, the ethically challenged FBI Assistant Director now being investigated for Hatch Act and other violations concerning the Clinton sponsorship of his wife's campaign against Virginia Senator Richard Black, led the Eurasian task force early in his career and has maintained contacts ever since. Many believe that McCabe was Steele's FBI handler and contact.

Although the public record of the doings of Fusion GPS is sparse, more can be gleaned from the fact that Fusion GPS principal Glenn Simpson lists himself as a Senior Fellow at the neocon International Assessment and Strategy Center (IASC), specializing in "corruption and transnational crime," a current preoccupation of the internationalized FBI which Robert Mueller created. IASC's President is Thor Ronay, formerly Vice-President of Frank Gaffney's Center for Security Policy. Kenneth deGraffenreid is the senior fellow for intelligence policy.

Executive Order 12333, partially authored by Kenneth deGraffenreid during the Reagan Administration, allows U.S. intelligence agencies, including the FBI

---

2. A Russian "tech expert" who operates the global tech firm XBT Holding.

3. An investigation which claimed that Russia secured the 2018 World Cup as a result of bribes, alleging deep relationships between FIFA (*Fédération Internationale de Football Association*) and Russian organized crime.

and CIA, to outsource operations to "private entities" like Fusion GPS and Orbis, and then to deny the resulting relationship. It also governs most of the surveillance activities conducted by U.S. agencies domestically and throughout the globe, and allows responsible officials to deny such activities.

In the May 17, 2017 court filing, Christopher Steele and Orbis outline their attempts to influence the U.S. election by smearing Donald Trump as a Russian agent on behalf of Hillary Clinton's candidacy. They state that, in September 2016, they briefed reporters from the *New York Times*, the *Washington Post*, the *New Yorker*, Yahoo News, and CNN about Christopher Steele's reports on Trump and Russia, and participated in further briefings with the *New York Times*, the *Washington Post*, and Yahoo News in October 2016. In late October, Steele briefed a reporter from *Mother Jones* via Skype. Senator John McCain and David Kramer, who was McCain's agent, were briefed on the pre-election Steele memoranda in December 2016, according to the filing. Sixteen such memoranda were produced prior to the election. It seems otherwise clear that the FBI was also a recipient of all of these memoranda, dating back to June 2016, if not earlier.

Steele and Orbis claim that the seventeenth memo, produced in December 2016, which referenced Gubarev and the salacious and disgusting claim that Trump engaged in perverse sexual activities at a Russian hotel, was solely produced to David Kramer,[4] Senator John McCain, and a representative of the British security services. The December memo was the product of a collaboration between Steele, Sir Andrew Wood, Kramer, and a representative of the British security services, which began on November 18, 2017—that is, almost immediately following Trump's election as president. Previously, David Kramer had held State Department positions dedicated to Project Democracy. Project Democracy and its various offshoots, based on agreements between President Reagan and British Prime Minister Margaret Thatcher, is the well-known mechanism for producing coups, rigged elections, and regime change in countries which fall into imperial disfavor. It seems clear that in order to save themselves in the British lawsuit, Steele and Orbis are trying to make John McCain and David Kramer the fall guys for their actions.

---

4. Kramer is the former President of the CIA and NED quango, Freedom House, a fellow of the Project for a New American Century, and a close ally of John McCain.

The Non-Existent Russian 'Hack' of the DNC

According to a January 2017 report on Russian hacking, issued by Barack Obama's Director of National Intelligence (DNI) James Clapper, the Russians were inside the DNC computer servers by July 2015; the DNC was notified, but did nothing about it for over a year. British press, including the *Guardian*, state that British intelligence warned its U.S. counterparts of the Russian hack of the DNC in July 2015, but somehow could not gain their attention. By December 2015, according to Clapper's report, hundreds of paid Russian trolls associated with the St. Petersburg, Russia, Internet Research Agency (IRA) had begun to advocate for Trump's election. Stories about alleged new modes of Russian propaganda involving the Internet and social media had appeared in the British press throughout 2014-2015, including British claims about the Internet Research Agency, but only surfaced prominently in the United States after the issuance of Clapper's report. The citation of the IRA is yet another large British fingerprint on the hacking hoax.

On November 24, 2016, a mysterious entity called *Propaganda or Not?* produced a list of two hundred Internet sites that had allegedly been tasked by the Kremlin with relaying Russian propaganda and intoxicating U.S. public opinion, to the point that they elected Donald Trump. They included just about every site with a record of opposition to the new Cold War, whether on the right or left of the so-called political spectrum, and/or opposition more generally to Anglo-American geopolitical permanent warfare policies. The *Washington Post's* production of this list set off a campaign by various new entities, including one proposed for the U.S. State Department by Congress and Obama in the 2016 National Defense Authorization Act, to censor the news by blacklisting and de-legitimizing these websites. According to French journalist Thierry Meyssan, *Propaganda or Not?* unites *Polygraph*, a Voice of America (VOA) site; the *Interpreter*, a magazine of Mikhail Khodorkovsky's Institute for Modern Russia; the Center for European Policy Analysis; and Alperovitch's Digital Forensics Service.

In March 2017, in what must be viewed as a national embarrassment, U.S. Senators on the Select Committee on Intelligence Activities listened—in seemingly amazed, mesmerized wonder—as Thomas Rid of King's College, London, Roy Godson, and other British-schooled intelligence experts told them that thousands of paid Russian trolls had infiltrated the American mind with Russian-generated conspiracy theories and swung the election to Donald Trump. The seemingly brain-dead Senators embraced this narrative wholeheartedly.

All of this anti-Russia frenzy, of course, finds its supposed justification in the original claim by CrowdStrike of Russian hacking of DNC servers. Yet, on July 24, 2017, the Veterans Intelligence Professionals for Sanity (VIPS) released a *Memorandum to the President*, demonstrating that *there was no Russian hack* of the DNC. Rather, the original WikiLeaks document trove was produced by a leak from inside the DNC, not a hack. According to the VIPS memo, a second and subsequent leak from the DNC was altered in a "cut and paste" job to make it look like it was the product of a very crude Russian hack, brazenly leaving "Russian" fingerprints all over the fabrication, and done in such a way as to both discredit the initial leak, and to present a false narrative of Russian interference in the U.S. Presidential election. The VIPS are veterans of U.S. intelligence agencies, and include William Binney, the former technical director of the NSA. They originally banded together to oppose the fabricated reasons for the Iraq War. You can see the complete interview of former CIA Officer Ray McGovern, conducted by LaRouche PAC's Jason Ross, about the VIPS memo here.

In their memo, the VIPS point to the CIA's "Marble Framework," an anti-forensic computer framework which allows for obfuscation of cyberattacks, and false flag attribution by the CIA. Thus the source code for any given malware program can be replaced with another language. This then gives CIA malware the appearance of having originated from one of these language-groups, as a means to throw off forensic investigators.

The Trump Tower Meeting

Undoubtedly, by the time of the June 9, 2016 Trump Tower meeting, the British government's Trump File was already overflowing with potential ammunition to use against candidate Trump, including a full history of Donald Trump's sponsorship of the 2013 Miss Universe pageant in Moscow; Trump's real estate dealings with Russians anywhere in the world; all of candidate

---

The 'Russian Agent' Smear Campaign

The targeting of the activities of the Internet Research Agency in the January 2017 DNI's report shows this aspect of the so-called Russian Active Measures campaign against Hillary Clinton to be a fiction, with deep roots in a British-created NATO intelligence operation called the Strategic Communications Service (SCA). From its inception, the SCA incorporated a service of the Atlantic Council, the Digital Forensics Service. CrowdStrike's Dimitri Alperovitch is, as previously stated, a senior fellow in this project.

According to French journalist Thierry Meyssan, as part of this operation, in September 2014, the British government created the 77th Brigade, a unit tasked with countering foreign propaganda, which worked with the U.S. military in Europe to interfere with websites considered to be distributing Russian propaganda. In the U.S., the Washington Center for European Policy Analysis created the Information Warfare Initiative, also to counter alleged Russian propaganda, with heavy support from the Khodorkovsky family's Institute of Modern Russia in New York. Mikhail Khodorkovsky is an exiled Russian oligarch who plotted a coup against Vladimir Putin on behalf of his western backers, who include London's Lord Rothschild, George Soros, and the Bush family. The *Washington Post*'s neocon Anne Applebaum is cited by Meyssan as the creator of the Information Warfare Initiative.

The Center for European Policy Analysis is a pseudopod of the National Endowment for Democracy and the U.S. intelligence community. It has concentrated its attacks on the Russian broadcasters *RT* and *Sputnik*, which of course, became central targets of DNI Clapper's phony January 2017 report on Russian hacking. Most analysts say that the first target of this NATO campaign was countering any news or person favorable to the Russian position concerning Ukraine, or any news revealing the Nazi proclivities of the persons the U.S. State Department supported in its Ukrainian regime-change operation.

Donald Trump, Jr.

Trump's conciliatory statements toward Russia; complaints that campaign advisor Michael Flynn was soft on Russia and a rebel against the U.S. intelligence establishment from within that establishment; and surveillance of Trump's campaign manager, Paul Manafort, who was considered an outright enemy of Anglo-American interests, given his political work for the former President of Ukraine, Victor Yanukovych and his Party of the Regions. As previously mentioned, Yanukovych was ousted in the Ukrainian coup directed by the National Endowment for Democracy (NED), the U.S. State Department's Victoria Nuland, and Barack Obama, which reversed the results of an election previously certified as free and fair by all Western observers. In addition, Carter Page, who volunteered for the Trump campaign as a foreign policy walk-in, had a variety of business dealings in Russia and had already functioned as an FBI informant in a major FBI case against Russian organized crime figures.

The official British government file also probably included reports and photos from surveillance of apartments at Trump Tower associated with a then-ongoing investigation of a Russian organized crime ring said to operate there. Individuals involved in the FIFA corruption investigation also lived there. The FIFA investigation was worked by the FBI Eurasian Organized Crime Strike Force and Christopher Steele.

So, before the crazy email setting up the Trump Tower meeting, and setting up Donald Trump, Jr., is

even sent, we already have the following intelligence services in motion and attempting to concoct illicit dirt about Trump and Putin: British intelligence; Ukrainian intelligence; the Office of the Director of National Intelligence (ODNI), the FBI, and the CIA in the United States; and NATO's Strategic Communications and its U.S. offshoots. But even that's not everybody involved. According to *Foreign Policy* magazine and others, on July 11, 2017, a hacker going by the name of "Johnnie Walker" published a trove of emails from the private account of Robert Otto, an individual tasked to a secretive unit in the U.S. State Department focused on Russia. *Newsweek* magazine states that Otto is the nation's "foremost" intelligence expert concerning Russia. To date, those emails have not been authenticated; however, they contain an email—purported to be on the day of the Trump Tower meeting—between Otto and Kyle Parker, staffer on the House Committee on Foreign Affairs, featuring a picture of Russian attorney Natalia Veselnitskaya's house in Russia. Parker acclaims himself as the actual author of the Magnitsky Act sanctions against Russia and a close friend of Bill Browder. Veselnitskaya claims that her children have been threatened as a result of her participation in a legal case questioning the bona fides of Bill Browder and the foundations of the Magnitsky Act.

The picture of her house suggests yet another level of intelligence community surveillance and involvement with the Trump Tower meeting.

The Set-Up

On June 3, 2016, Donald Trump, Jr. received an email from publicist Ron Goldstone, a former British tabloid journalist who now operates out of the United States. Goldstone's Facebook account appears to indicate that he is presently on a break from his businesses and on a world tour of gay bathhouses, in which the proudly obese Goldstone takes pictures of himself wearing various strange hats and shirts in the company of young men. Who is financing this tour apparently outside the reach of Grand Jury subpoenas? Goldstone has also been photographed with the actress and stand-up comic Kathy Griffin, who famously posted a picture of herself with President Trump's severed head.

Here is the pertinent content from the first email:

Natalia Veselnitskaya

The Crown prosecutor of Russia met with … Aras this morning and in their meeting offered to provide the Trump campaign with some official documents and information that would incriminate Hillary and her dealings with Russia and would be very useful to your father. This is obviously very high level and sensitive information but is *part of Russia and its government's support for Mr. Trump—helped along by Aras and Emin.*[5] [Emphasis added]

Aras is Aras Agalarov. Emin is his son, a Russian billionaire who brought the Miss Universe pageant to Moscow.

There is no "Crown prosecutor of Russia." The position does not exist. A Radio Free Europe, Radio

Liberty Release of May 19, 2016, does point out that the Prosecutor General, Yuri Chaika, was pursuing a violation of U.S. laws involving $37 million in taxes due to the Russian government by William Browder, Browder's U.S. lawyer Jamison Firestone, and the Ziff Brothers, a New York firm long associated with William Browder. On June 4, Chaika told a national Russian television audience that he had presented this claim to U.S. authorities for action. The Ziffs and Browder were contributors to the Clinton Global Initiative. Chaika and the Russian government have otherwise campaigned very publicly for repeal of Magnitsky Act sanctions against Russians, calling them the product of a scam and a fraud by Bill Browder. We will treat Browder much more fully below. But, as previously noted, Browder is also a big-time representative of London financial and intelligence interests.

The actual twenty-minute Trump Tower meeting involved Russian attorney Natalia Veselnitskaya, who did most of the speaking by all accounts; Rinat Akhmetshin, a well-known Washington, D.C.-based lobbyist and American citizen; Ike Kaveladze, a U.S. citizen and vice-president at one of the Agalarovs' companies; Ron Goldstone; and the translator for Natalia Veselnitskaya, Anatoli Samochornov. Samochornov is also an American citizen who worked with Veselnitskaya frequently, since she does not speak English. He has also worked extensively for the FBI and the U.S. State Department. None of these people have "Putin's ear" or present apparent connections to Russian intelligence. Although Akhmetshin has been "linked" to Russian counterintelligence repeatedly in the news media, that all appears to be based on his bragging about his two-year stint as a young man in the Russian military.

Any sound investigation would focus on who, out of the small army of intelligence operatives watching this meeting, designed and implemented the clear entrapment attempt against Donald Trump, Jr., for later use. Since it was surveilled and recorded by multiple intelligence agencies, probably tripping all over one another at the time like Keystone Cops, why was the Trump Tower meeting only surfaced as the "smoking gun" recently? Goldstone's first email to Trump reads like any planted FBI missive or planted evidence, awkward and inconsistent in its own internal content—"your father," "Mr. Trump," and "Aras and Emin are working for the Russian government, and they are working on your

---

5. Aras Agalarov and Emin Agalarov partnered with Trump for the 2013 Miss Universe pageant in Moscow. Emin is an Azerbaijani pop star whose publicist is Ron Goldstone. According to a very useful article (see https://www.bloomberg.com/view/articles/2017-07-11/trump-s-low-level-russian-connection) in *Bloomberg News*, they are not particularly close to Putin, although they are major builders in Russia. Their base of operations is the Moscow regional government. Stating that individuals who operate at this level in Russia have Putin's ear would be equivalent to saying that the Bronx Borough President was implementing foreign policy on behalf of the U.S. President.

behalf on this sensitive and official matter, and I am putting that in an email." Trump Jr. and others say that no opposition research about Clinton was offered at the meeting, which instead focused on the Byzantine intrigue which is the international battle about the Magnitsky Act. Trump Jr. obviously couldn't follow the dense threads and found the discussion "inane."

Veselnitskaya, herself, had been paroled into the United States to serve as the Russian lawyer for the Russian businessman Denis Katsyv in a bizarre legal proceeding brought by former U.S. Attorney Preet Bharara in the Southern District of New York, based solely on allegations made by Bill Browder concerning the tax fraud allegations that led to the U.S. Magnitsky Act. At the time of the Trump Tower meeting, however, Veselnitskaya was traveling on a business visa issued by the U.S. Department of State, after having previously been denied such a visa, and after efforts by the U.S. Attorney for the Southern District of New York to prevent any free travel by her in the United States at all. Immigration attorneys I have spoken with say this situation is unusual, "strange."

Following the Trump Tower meeting, Veselnitskaya, Akhmetshin, and Samochornov were involved in the showing of a film critical of Bill Browder by Andrei Nekrasov, at the Newseum in Washington, D.C. on June 13, as well as in lobbying Congress against the Magnitsky Act. The Newseum showing of Nekrasov's anti-Browder film was emceed by renowned investigative reporter Seymour Hersh.

On July 15, 2016, at the same time that James Comey opened an FBI investigation of "Russian interference in the U.S. election," Bill Browder's Hermitage Capital Management filed a complaint with the Justice Department accusing a plethora of individuals of violating the Foreign Agents Registration Act, including Akhmetshin, Veselnitskaya, Samochornov, Chris Cooper (a former *Wall Street Journal* reporter and leader of the Potomac Square Group, a Washington, D.C. lobbying firm), former Democratic Congressman Ron Dellums, Howard Schweitzer of Cozens, O'Connor Public Strategies, and Glenn Simpson of Fusion GPS. Browder claims that all were involved directly in a campaign steered by Putin himself to overturn the Mag-

William Browder

nitsky Act sanctions against Russia and to kill the 2016 legislative expansion of the Magnitsky Act in the U.S. Congress.

The Bill Browder File

To hear Browder tell it,—in his Congressional testimony on July 27, in countless performances throughout the world, and in his book, *Red Notice*—Bill Browder, the grandson of Earl Browder, the General Secretary of the Communist Party U.S.A., is a super-savvy investor who made a fortune in Russia from the middle 1990s until 2005. Bill championed anti-corruption measures, such as shareholders' values, and initially had Putin's backing in "name-and-shame" campaigns leading to the cleaning up the image of certain companies including Yukos, the state oil enterprise. Suddenly, Browder alleges, Putin turned on him and banned him from Russia in 2005 as a threat to state security. Thereafter, a Russian criminal gang, functioning out of the Interior Ministry and the Federal Security Service (FSB), deployed to steal Browder's companies out from under him, resulting in a tax fraud against the Russian government to the tune of $230 million. Putin is in on all of this, says Browder, because he has deals with Russia's criminal mafia and oligarchs which have made him the world's richest man and is himself a heartless, ruthless, and cold-blooded murderer. Anyone voicing a different view is an "enabler" of murder, including former U.S. Secretary of State John Kerry, whom Browder calls a "Putin lackey." That's the "narrative," according to Browder.

Also, as Browder tells it, his Russian "lawyer," Sergei Magnitsky, blew the whistle on the tax fraud scheme, was jailed by Putin as a result, and died in jail in 2009 after being denied medical attention, tortured, and finally beaten to death by Russian prison guards. In 2012, the U.S. Congress, led by Senators John McCain and Ben Cardin, working through Kyle Parker, wrote sanctions against the Russians who Browder claims were involved in Magnitsky's death, banning their travel and their use of financial institutions. Despite Secretary Kerry's opposition, President Obama signed

EIRNS/Rachel Douglas

During the looting of Russia in the 1990s, many Russians were reduced to digging in the trash.

these sanctions into law. Russia responded by banning the adoption of Russian children in the United States and sanctioning various U.S. officials involved in the War on Iraq. Hence Donald Trump, Jr.'s initial statement that he remembered the Trump Tower meeting to be about Russian adoptions.

Even minimal research shows that Browder's narrative cannot possibly hold water. Our own, initial, research into Bill Browder's story, mostly following leads from his own account in *Red Notice*, indicates that his "career" shows all of the characteristics of a sponsored deep-penetration agent, acting in an intelligence and operational capacity for the the very same Anglo-American interests that looted and destroyed the Russian economy in the 1990s and early 2000s. The destruction of Russia's economy was an entirely deliberate Anglo-American wrecking operation engineered through Thatcherite "shock therapy," with a helping hand from economists Larry Summers and Jeffrey Sachs. This led to control of the ruined economy and state enterprises by Russian oligarchs, who acted as straw-men for Western financial and intelligence interests centered in the City of London. Their methods included the use of criminal gangs to facilitate wholesale looting of the state and the population.

During this period, Mr. Browder portrays himself as a super "lone entrepreneur," making millions for undisclosed clients, buying and selling former state assets, and all the while not speaking a word of Russian. He claims that he became an *uber* capitalist buccaneer in reaction to his Communist grandfather and his mathematician parents. Recently he has claimed that he renounced his American citizenship and became a British citizen because his grandmother was harassed during the McCarthy period. More skeptical observers say it was to avoid U.S. taxes.

The average lifespan of the Russian male declined to fifty-four years as a result of the Anglo-American assault, the former economic infrastructure of the country was sold at basement prices to Western interests, the country was flooded with drugs, the population suffered negative growth rates, Russian scientists and engineers fled the country, and millions suffered completely unnecessary deaths. This was a foreign-imposed policy of calculated economic genocide. While there are many books documenting this process, we only note here that the ultimate Anglo-American goal was to split Russia into three separate countries and prevent it from ever again functioning as a nation-state, while taking Western ownership of the country's huge natural resources. Vladimir Putin stopped all of this and began the process of rebuilding Russia. That is the real reason

Putin is demonized by the British and their allies in Washington and Wall Street, and why Browder paints himself as Putin's Number One enemy.

Browder's investment career begins with an apprenticeship at an investment company owned by British mega-publisher Robert Maxwell. Maxwell has been named in accounts too numerous to mention, as a joint British-Israeli spy, and as a double agent for the British with the Russians. According to recently released documents, he carried a request by Mikhail Gorbachov to Margaret Thatcher in 1990, for a $20 billion loan in order to continue the British policy of *perestroika* as the Russian economy began to fall part. Maxwell famously looted millions of dollars from the pension funds of the employees of his British publishing empire. He died by somehow falling off his yacht in the midst of his companies' financial distress.

Browder next ended up on the Russia desk of Salomon Brothers in London after his sojourn with Maxwell. Readers of the Wall Street confessional, *Liar's Poker,* will immediately see the implications of that. Browder even makes a self-conscious reference to *Liar's Poker* in his own account, while attempting to distance himself from what has been publicly acknowledged to have been a nest of outright thievery. At Salomon Brothers, Browder discovers that he can make millions of dollars buying Russia assets, which are valued dirt cheap under Yeltsin's privatization pro-

---

Browder and Safra

Browder cites Edmond Safra as his "mentor" and closest confidant, as well as his Russian business partner.

Safra, who was murdered in an arson fire in 1999, was perhaps the king of worldwide money laundering for political intelligence purposes, at TD Bank (a subsidiary of Toronto-Dominion Bank in Canada) and at Republic Bank of New York. In 1989, the Drug Enforcement Administration (DEA) and U.S. Customs linked Republic and Safra to major money laundering schemes by the Medellín Cartel and a Swiss company that was a laundromat for Syrian and East Bloc heroin profits. TD Bank and Safra also played a role in the George H.W. Bush/Oliver North Iran Contra drug and money laundering operations. In 1996, Robert Friedman published an extraordinary article in *New York* magazine entitled, "The Money Plane." Five nights a week, crisp, uncirculated, $100 bills were being flown by the planeload from JFK International Airport nonstop to Moscow where the money became part of the Russian mafia's vast international crime syndicate operations then engaged in brutally looting and cannibalizing the former Soviet Union. According to an official of the Federal Comptroller of the Currency, cited by Robert Friedman, "That money is used to support organized crime: It is used to support black market operations.

... In my personal opinion it is an absolute abomination."

The Money Plane operation accounted for more than $40 billion dollars pumped into Russian organized crime between 1994-1996, and the players were Safra's Republic National Bank of New York and the New York Federal Reserve. Various officials in the United States did not even try to dispute Friedman's account. Instead, they covered up its implications in public relations horsepucky. The coverup was led by none other than U.S. Senator, then Congressman, Charles Schumer (NY). In the first two years after the Soviet Union's collapse, an estimated $60 to $70 billion worth of material assets—weapons, oil, gold, and artwork, were outright stolen out of the country by organized crime networks on the receiving end of freshly printed U.S. dollars. For the bank participation in this scheme, Safra's bank earned a huge fee. Far more profitable, however, was actually the moving and laundering of dirty money by buying Russia assets. For that, Safra required ground troops in Russia, which suggests the actual role of Browder and Hermitage under his tutelage. Maybe that's why Browder had security in Russia consisting of former British and Mossad agents. Others have speculated that Safra and his assets, including Browder, were the major backers of the Russian oligarch, Boris Berezovsky. According to Russian reports, Berezovsky sought to end his own exile by producing documents showing that Browder was an MI6 and CIA agent code-named "Solomon."

---

grams. But, allegedly, he can't get Salomon to fully recognize his brilliance, so he decides to strike out on his own.

Somehow, Benny Steinmetz, the Israeli diamond billionaire and Edmond Safra, the British/Israeli financier and intelligence agent,—both major players in the world of dirty finance—appear out of the blue in Browder's story, and invest in his company, Hermitage Capital Management, to the tune of $25 million. That is it concerning what Browder discloses about his investors. The $25 million is a fairly paltry operating fund for someone who claims to have ended up being Russia's largest foreign investor.

Stranger still, even before the Safra investment, we learn from Browder's account that he is co-hosting major events at the World Economic Forum at Davos and receiving confidences from former Russian Finance Minister Boris Fyodorov, this while he is still, purportedly, an unknown thirty-something Moscow businessman.

It is clear that Browder and Safra profited initially from the entirely corrupt "loans for shares" program under Yeltsin, which resulted in the looting of former state assets by foreign, mostly British interests. "Shaming" and "Naming" campaigns are, of course, hostile takeover techniques perfected by the City of London and Wall Street, and a powerful weapon used to gain assets at an artificially depressed price.

Following Safra's 1999 murder, Browder's next sponsor and administrator for Hermitage was the Swiss private branch of the Hongkong and Shanghai Banking Corporation. HSBC is perhaps the most corrupt banking and intelligence operation in human history. HSBC is a strategic asset of the British oligarchy. Famously, HSBC was founded to launder the dope money pouring in from Britain's opium war against China. Ever since, HSBC has not deviated at all from criminal activity, and has been cited repeatedly in the United States and abroad for drug-money laundering, terrorist arms financing, and other black-market activities. HSBC's most recent dustup with U.S. authorities involved a 2012 deferred prosecution agreement signed off on by the Department of Justice after HSBC was found to have laundered millions of dollars for Mexico's Sinaloa drug cartel.

Former FBI Director Comey joined HSBC's Board to supervise this agreement shortly before being appointed as FBI Director. The Justice Department argued that HSBC's continued operation was necessary for the stability of the world's financial system, against strident internal opposition from investigators in the case who insisted the HSBC must be shut down. On February 9, 2015, the International Consortium of Investigative Journalists released leaked documents showing that HSBC Private Bank (Suisse), Browder's exact partner in Hermitage, serviced a mix of "tax-dodging plutocrats, dictators' bagmen, blood diamond dealers, cocaine traffickers, and Al Qaeda financiers," in the words of the *Washington Post*.

To finish out the deep British pedigree, Browder states that no one less than Tony Blair himself—the Prime Minister—was prepared to raise the issue with Putin himself, of getting Browder's passport back, at the G8 summit in 2006.

The Magnitsky Myth

> It is 100% permissible—bordering on obligatory—to spout the most insane, evidence-free conspiracy theories if they involve Russia and Putin.
>
> —Glenn Greenwald

In 2013, Preet Bhahara, the U.S. Attorney for the Southern District of New York, brought a legal action against Prevezon Holdings and related companies, and Denis Katsyv (Case No. 1:13-cv-06326, U.S. v. Prevezon Holdings, et al.). The case sought forfeiture of assets from Prevezon and other companies associated with the Katsyv family in Russia, based on the allegation that these companies had laundered some of the funds from the $230 million tax theft alleged by Browder. The Russian government's position has consistently been that Browder engaged in tax fraud in Russia, that his companies were under investigation from 2002 forward for this fraud, and that Magnitsky, Browder's long-time accountant, had come up with schemes to facilitate the fraud. Browder was convicted *in absentia* of tax fraud by Russia in 2013. The Russians have also alleged that Browder used proxy Russian purchasers to illegally attempt to take a major position in Gazprom, the oil company that is considered to be a state asset. They also suspect that Browder himself was involved in engineering the tax fraud against their government in order to deflect from his own crimes.

The Homeland Security case agent in the Prevezon case testified that the government's case was based solely on Browder's account, and that he "hoped" a

Grand Jury convened by the U.S. attorney, and the case itself, would produce sufficient evidence to back the Browder/U.S. government claims. Normally, in U.S. legal proceedings, the evidence is largely in hand before a case is filed, and criminal grand jury proceedings are not convened to support a civil proceeding. The Katsyv family interests are long-time Russian clients of Natalia Veselnitskaya, the Russian lawyer in the Trump Jr. meeting.

The case was settled after extensive pre-trial litigation, with about $6 million being paid to the U.S. Treasury by the defendants. How an alleged fraud against the Russian treasury ends up in the U.S. Treasury is a remarkable phenomenon. There was no admission of wrongdoing by the Russian defendants. Both sides declared victory. It is noteworthy that Browder's companies were not harmed by the alleged fraud—he had already spirited his profits out of Russia at the time he was barred. Rather, Browder and the United States attempted to claim that the Hongkong and Shanghai Banking Corporation was the victim of the fraud alleged by Browder.

Facts emerging from this case—and the documentary film prepared by Putin critic cum Browder critic Andrei Nekrasov—have caused many, even in the mainstream U.S. media, to review the narrative expounded by Browder. See, for example the NBC News story of July 24, 2017, the "Legal Battle Behind the Trump Tower Meeting," questioning Browder's account of Magnitsky's death and noting a finding by Judge William H. Pauley III in the Prevezon case that a 2013 Council of Europe report on the Magnitsky case was unreliable because it did not fairly examine both sides of the controversy.

Based on what we have set forth here, which is readily available to anyone with a degree of research skill and patience, why did the U.S. Senate Judiciary Committee give Bill Browder a full two hours to spout his anti-Putin tirade on July 27, treating him as a human rights hero? According to accounts of Browder's deposition in the Prevezon case, he was confronted by evidence proving that Sergei Magnitsky was his longtime accountant and not a lawyer. Magnitsky was deeply implicated in devising various schemes for Browder to avoid Russian taxes, including using disabled Russian citizens as straw shareholders. Magnitsky had been questioned about this and other tax irregularities by the Russian Interior Ministry in 2006,

far ahead of the 2007 date when Browder said he first hired him. According to the Russians, Magnitsky was not arrested because he was the whistleblower on the $230 million fraud against the Russian treasury, but because he was implicated in Browder's own tax fraud. The Russians say that Magnitsky did die tragically in a Russian jail because of medical neglect, but insist that he was not beaten to death as alleged by Browder.

There were also huge holes in Browder's story about the alleged $230 million fraud against the Russian treasury. According to accounts of Browder's deposition in the Prevezon case, he claimed fifty times that he couldn't remember details about the story he has told millions of times, and constantly deferred to "his team," and to a trove of purloined documents gathered in violation of Russian and other privacy laws. Browder answered "I don't know," a full two hundred eleven times. It was the first time Browder had been subjected to cross-examination of his story, as he has repeatedly avoided legal process.

As for the discrepancies flowing from Andrei Nekrasov's film about Browder, we can't tell you about them first hand, because Browder, his National Endowment for Democracy congressional and lobbyist cronies, and his British protectors, have waged a worldwide campaign to prevent the film from being shown. Lawsuits from Browder have greeted any distribution company willing to show the film. When the film was shown at the Newseum, in Washington, D.C., in June 2016, shortly after the Trump Tower meeting, Kyle Parker, Browder's House Foreign Affairs Committee handler, and others of his ilk, organized to disrupt the showing. And, the showing of the film itself is part of Browder's Justice Department claim that those who organized the showing had to register under the Foreign Agents Registration Act. Yet, Browder himself used many of Washington's most powerful lobbyists to sell his dubious story to Congress, tapping for the task such luminaries as Jonathan Winer of APCO Worldwide and Juleanna Glover—Dick Cheney's former spokeswoman, press aide to candidate John McCain, and lobbying partner to former Attorney General John Ashcroft.

So, folks, that's just the deep British pedigree to events in one month, June 2016, events which are cardinal, seminal, to the ongoing coup—and existential as to the future of our Republic. When will the nation find the guts to take up Lyndon LaRouche's call: "Stop the Coup, Cancel the British, Save the People!"?

'Cancel the British Empire To Stop World War and Save the People'

The following is an edited version of a presentation given by Will Wertz, a member of the Editorial Board of EIR, *to the Manhattan Town Hall meeting of LaRouche PAC, on Aug. 5, 2017. A* video *of that entire meeting is available.*

I'm going to start out with a comment that Lyndon LaRouche made earlier this week. LaRouche said, "The American people must demand that the ongoing treasonous British coup against the U.S. Presidency and the nation itself, must be stopped and its perpetrators prosecuted and imprisoned. The British system must be cancelled, and the President must make every effort to save the people of this country and the rest of humanity from further British-directed depravations against their lives. Cancel the British system; save the people!"

What I want to do today is to address the role of the British government in the current coup against the Presidency and in a general policy of subversion of the United States as a nation, of our Constitution, going back any number of years.

The way I'll begin is by addressing the coup against the Presidency. Crucial in the fight against this coup is the VIPS [Veteran Intelligence Professionals for Sanity] statement, which is put out by the steering committee of their organization. They are all top-level former intelligence officials. LaRouche PAC did an interview with Ray McGovern, who is on that steering committee, published on our website just recently. What they did is the first forensic analysis of the so-called "Russian hack." What they established is based on the postings of the data—they did not have access to the actual computer of the DNC; what they established is that physically it could not have been carried out over the Internet, because the Internet is physically incapable of

> **"The so-called 'Russian hack': … it could not have been carried out over the Internet, because the Internet is physically incapable of downloading the volume of data in the time that it took. … this was an inside job"**

downloading the volume of data in the time that it took. So therefore, as WikiLeaks and others have maintained, this was an inside job in which the emails were downloaded onto some type of data carrier—a thumb drive, or similar device. The second point is that this second intervention into the DNC computer system deliberately left footprints which would direct the investigation towards a Russian hack. As WikiLeaks recently exposed, in releasing information they called Vault VII, the CIA under Brennan developed a capability of falsely attributing a hack to another country—specifically Russia. They name a number of others that had the capability of doing that.

What these former U.S. intelligence officials argue, is that this was not a hack by the Russians; it was falsely attributed to the Russians after the fact. It was actually a leak carried out by a DNC insider. They say that they are prepared to defend this conclusion; they call on President Trump to speak to Pompeo at the CIA to get to the bottom of this. What we are also calling for, is that with Trump taking such action, there be an investigation in the U.S. Congress in which members of the VIPS are called to testify. The forensic evidence, presented by the VIPS, blows out of the water the fundamental hysterical assumption which lies at the base of the attack on President Trump, and also the sanctions bill, which was just passed into law, which is unconstitutional.

The Attack on Trump Originated in London

Let me just go back to the British role in this entire attack on the Presidency. Donald Trump announced his candidacy for the Presidency on June 16, 2015. An article appeared in the *Guardian*, on April 13, 2017—after Judge Napolitano had argued that Obama had ar-

Aerial view of the GCHQ in Cheltenham, Gloucestershire.

ranged for British Intelligence's GCHQ to surveil Trump—which says that GCHQ first became aware, in late 2015, of suspicious interactions between figures connected to Trump and known or suspected Russian agents. So, this surveillance of Trump, by British Intelligence, began within a matter of months after he announced his candidacy for the Presidency. GCHQ is Government Communications Headquarters; it's the British equivalent of the NSA in the United States. Judge Napolitano was more or less disinvited from appearing on Fox News after he made that claim. But the *Guardian* published on April 13, 2017, an article entitled, "British Spies Were First to Spot Trump Team's Links with Russia."

The *Guardian* article is very funny, defensively reporting, "It is understood that GCHQ was at no point carrying out a targeted operation against Trump or his team, or pro-actively seeking information. The alleged conversations were picked up by chance." [laughter] All right. Now, what's reported is that in 2016, Hannigan, the head of GCHQ, went directly to Brennan of the CIA, and informed him of so-called "intelligence" that had been gathered by GCHQ and most likely by MI-6, the British foreign intelligence agency – the equivalent of the CIA. What's reported is that as a result of Hannigan coming and speaking to Brennan, Brennan initiated a multi-agency U.S. intelligence investigation of Trump. This is in August 2016 in the middle of the Pres-

idential campaign. Brennan also briefed the "Gang of 8," the leading members of the House and Senate Intelligence Committees, and the Congressional leadership of both parties. So, the Republicans and Democrats are being briefed by Brennan on the basis of intelligence gathered by a foreign intelligence agency—GCHQ —against a Presidential campaign, in the middle of the campaign. And of course the investigation which was launched by Brennan involved the FBI, the NSA, and CIA. One wonders whether it's within the charter of the CIA to be launching investigations domestically against a U.S. President.

It's also reported in this *Guardian* article that Britain's MI-6 spy agency played a part in intelligence sharing with the U.S. So, you have both GCHQ and MI-6 involved in this operation; which is why Helga Zepp-LaRouche has pointed out that the real collusion is between the Obama administration and their intelligence agency stooges, like Brennan, Comey, and Clapper, with British Intelligence.

People should remember that John Brennan is the guy who would meet every Tuesday with the President to determine who was going to be killed that week; including extra-judicial assassinations of, in some cases, American citizens. John Brennan is the person who carried out illegal surveillance of the U.S. Senate Intelligence Committee when it was preparing a report on CIA torture, which he was complicit in. So, these two things should be understood.

What about Clapper? Clapper is the person who denied before the Senate Intelligence Committee that the NSA was engaged in surveillance of American citizens. He was asked the question by Senator [Ron] Wyden (D-OR), and he said, "No." Later on, when he was caught in having lied, he said "I said the least untruthful thing I could."

Now, we have an additional aspect to this, which is Christopher Steele, a so-called "former" agent of MI-6. We know from the *Guardian* article that MI-6 was also providing intelligence to the FBI and the CIA. Christopher Steele produced a dossier. He has a company called Orbis Business Intelligence, based in London.

He was hired by Fusion GPS, a U.S.-based company, and, allegedly, the report that he was commissioned to write, was paid for by supporters of Hillary Clinton. He put together this dossier, and then the dossier was given to the FBI, given to Brennan of the CIA, with unverified, slanderous material. But that report, to this day, remains the roadmap for the investigation being carried out by Mueller, the special counsel—and prior to that, by Comey.

When the campaign was coming to an end, the FBI entered into negotiations with Christopher Steele to pay him to continue his investigation. Orbis Business was founded in 2009, as was Fusion GPS. They have a confidentiality agreement which goes back to 2010, which means that the 2016 report was not the first engagement between Fusion GPS and Orbis. I would maintain that Fusion GPS is, in fact, operating as part of a British Intelligence operation against the U.S. Presidency. They argue, in response to Senator Grassley's request that they turn over information about the agreements to create this dossier, that they have a confidentiality agreement with Orbis; that's what they're trying to use to protect themselves.

The other figure in all this is the former acting director of the FBI. Because Christopher Wray was just confirmed, Andrew McCabe is no longer the acting director of the FBI. However he, when he began in the FBI, was the head of the Eurasian organized crime unit in New York City, from 2003 to 2006. Christopher Steele has admitted publicly that he was

Obama's Director of National Intelligence, James R. Clapper.

Former CIA Director John Brennan.

Andrew McCabe, Deputy Director of the FBI.

working with that unit, at least from the time period of 2010. So, what you have is a suspicion on the part of Grassley that it's Andrew McCabe who was involved in the discussions with Christopher Steele, including the discussions about paying him to continue his work. This is the nexus of real British Intelligence treason in the United States, operating against President Trump.

This is the result of the U.S.-British special relationship, so called. It should be noted that after World War II, in 1946, there was something called the U.S.-U.K. Agreement, which was set up to monitor the then-Soviet Union; but this agreement continues to this day, and is designed to monitor the former Soviet Union and Eastern Bloc nations. It eventually morphed into what's called the "Five Eyes," expanding from Britain and the United States to include Australia, New Zealand, and Canada. It is this apparatus which is involved in the surveillance of Trump. GCHQ is the centerpiece of this. GCHQ has about 5500 employees; that's the kind of operation you're talking about. Snowden, for instance, I think it was in 2013, exposed one of the programs of the Five Eyes called Echelon, which he emphasized is a *"supranational intelligence organization that doesn't answer to the known laws of its own countries."* So, they can use the excuse that the CIA or the NSA is not doing it, GCHQ is doing it, or another member of the Five Eyes; when in fact, the United States is directly involved in the entire surveillance operation.

British Lies on Syria

I'm going to use one other example of the British operation: the chemical weapons case in Syria. You have two of the biggest alleged crimes in modern history: the so-called hacking of the DNC computer and the chemical attack in Idlib Province, Syria, which became the basis for the U.S. launching a military attack on the Syrian airbase. In both of these cases, *the crime scene was never secured.* In both of these cases, *the crime scene was never investigated!* The DNC refused to allow the FBI to investigate their computer. We have been given this entire story about how the Russians hacked the DNC, but the FBI has never examined the computer. Similarly, the OPCW [Organization for Prohibition of Chemical Weapons] has never gone to the site of the alleged Syrian Air Force sarin attack.

I'm raising this chemical attack because it's further evidence of British involvement in operations against the United States. Sergey Lavrov, the Russian Foreign Minister, said, "I would like to remind you that we have pointed out a very strange coincidence, that the two groups of the OPCW fact-finding mission on the potential use of chemical weapons in Syria are chaired by U.K. citizens." Steven Wallis, a British subject, is the head of one of the fact-finding missions responsible for working with the Syrian government. Leonard Phillips, another British subject, works with the Syrian rebels. So, the investigation—to the extent which it occurred— took place under the responsibility of two U.K. subjects. It should be pointed out that not only was the site of the attack never investigated, but also the Syrians offered to bring investigators to the airfield, so that that could be investigated. If chemical weapons had been used from that site, it would have been evident; it couldn't have been hidden from the investigators—and neither of these things was done.

Remember that Idlib Province is controlled by al-Nusra, which is al-Qaeda; that's the excuse for not sending a UN delegation there to investigate—it's

UN/Jean-Marc Ferre

Carla Del Ponte, member of the UN Commission of Inquiry on Syria, addresses journalists in Geneva.

unsafe. We have also pointed out that the doctor from Idlib Province who was featured in all the news accounts, is a Dr. Shajul Islam, who happens to be a British doctor from the British National Health Service. In 2012, he was in Syria fighting with the jihadists against the Syrian government. When he returned to Britain, he was arrested because he was involved in the abduction of two journalists, one a British journalist and the other a Dutch journalist. But he was released without a trial going forward, and sent back to Syria. He then became the spokesman quoted in the media (CNN et al.), saying this was a Syrian government chemical attack. The NGO on the ground in all of these areas controlled by al-Nusra, is called the "White Helmets," which received $123 million, from 2013 to 2016, to build them up as an organization. They were founded by a British military agent by the name of James Le Mesurier, who was a graduate of the Royal Military Academy and a recipient of the Queen's Medal.

If you look at the OPCW report, they say the following: "At the time of handover" of so-called evidence, "the team was informed that all samples were taken by non-governmental organizations. A representative of an NGO was also interviewed and provided photographs and videos from the scene of the alleged incident." All the evidence came from the British-created White Helmets, which is the NGO that they're talking about.

I would also point out the following: There's a certain amnesia that takes place in terms of chemical weapons. In 2013, there was a chemical attack in East Ghouta. Carla Del Ponte went there as part of the UN investigative committee. She is quoted in the *Telegraph,* at that point, saying, "According to the testimonies we have gathered, the rebels have used chemical weapons, making use of sarin gas. It is, at the moment, opponents of the regime who are using sarin gas." She was also interviewed by Reuters, saying, "This was used on the part of the opposition, the rebels, not the government authority." So, we know that the rebels have access to sarin gas.

It's also reported by the OPCW that when the Syria government allowed its chemical weapons facilities to be dismantled and removed from the country, there were then twelve chemical weapons facilities; ten were removed. The other two were controlled by the rebels, so those were never removed.

British Intelligence and British Geopolitics

There's a very interesting book called, *Desperate Deception: British Covert Operations in the U.S. 1939-1944*, by Thomas Mahl. What it demonstrates, and this has been indicated in other publications as well, is that the British, starting in 1939, set up intelligence operations in the United States. Of course, this was a period in which Winston Churchill knew he needed the United States to defeat the Nazis: the Nazis had actually turned against Britain, after the British had helped create the Nazis in the first place. The British had an intelligence operation in the United States; it was centered here in New York at Rockefeller Center, and it was called the British Security Cooperation. It was located on the thirty-eighth floor of the International Building of the Rockefeller Center. William Stephenson represented MI6; he also represented MI5, and he ran the Special Operations Executive. He worked closely with what later became the CIA, and the person that he worked with was Allen Dulles. Allen Dulles operated out of Room 3663, 630 Fifth Avenue. The British Security Cooperation operated out of Room 3603, 630 Fifth Avenue. Stephenson also worked closely with "Gay" Edgar Hoover.

Let me just read you a couple of things. The British set up a forgery factory in Toronto, Canada for their war efforts. There was a memorandum which was released Nov. 26, 1941, called, "Atrocity Photographs." It says "they could quite easily provide a regular supply of 'atrocity pictures' manufactured by us in Canada, the buying and hiring of costumes, the manufacture of small pieces of scenery and of dummies, a first class make-up man—all of which could be carried out under some sort of cover." I mention that, because all of these videos they produce in Syria are just such "atrocity photos." In this case, they were trying to generate atrocity photos of atrocities carried out by the Nazis.

Roosevelt worked with Churchill, but Roosevelt, as reported by his son Elliott Roosevelt, told Churchill: "We're not fighting this war to preserve the British Empire... after this war, we want to develop the world with American system methods and dismantle your imperial system." But after Roosevelt's death, this is the apparatus that took over. As I said earlier, the U.S.-U.K. agreement was signed in 1946 under Truman. In a certain way, I would argue that the environment in the United States after Churchill launched the Cold War, with Trumanism and McCarthyism, creates precisely the kind of state of mind—pure terror—that you see today with the lemming-like group-think action on the part of the U.S. Congress and Senate on behalf of the sanctions bill—even though they should know that this is something that can lead to thermonuclear war.

I'm using those as two examples: The failure to investigate the DNC computer and the way the British operated in terms of this chemical incident in Syria—I'm using those to demonstrate the nature of the British operation, which should be transparent to everybody, except for the way that they've been trained to think.

We fought a revolution against the British. It's the British who burned down the White House. It's the British who were involved in the assassination of Hamilton and the assassination of Lincoln. One of the biggest shifts in U.S. policy orientation was after the assassination of McKinley. Before that, the United States was working with Russia, working with Germany. After McKinley's assassination, you had the Anglophile Teddy Roosevelt, who came in and shifted the entire policy. Over the past century—and into this century—what you've had is a shift toward the U.S.-British special relationship, as opposed to the traditional U.S. policy of working with other nations for economic development, that is, the American system of economics, which is coherent with what President Trump announced in a number of speeches in Kentucky and Detroit a month or two ago, and also coherent with his advocacy of Glass-Steagall.

The British know we are on the verge of a financial collapse. There was a very interesting interview with Alan Greenspan, who otherwise is not quotable. He pointed to the real danger of a bond bubble that could blow out very soon. Others have made similar types of warnings. We are on the verge of that. The British are still committed to maintaining their bankrupt imperial

Zbigniew Brzezinski

system. The British system is based on the Venetian system, which was a financial system. So those who argue "well, the British Empire doesn't exist anymore because they're not militarily occupying this and that country," miss the point. It is fundamentally a financial form of imperialism. You see the way in which, as Helga says, they have attempted to pull the United States into this British Empire, the "Commonwealth." The other four countries in the Five Eyes are all members of the British Commonwealth. The British tried to pull the United States into this arrangement. It is that arrangement that has to be destroyed. It has to be cancelled! As Lyndon LaRouche said.

The whole policy against Russia and China is a remake of the geopolitical doctrine of Harold Mackinder, who was a British geopolitical thinker who worked with [Karl] Haushofer of Germany, who was instrumental in designing Hitler's policy. In 1919, Halford Mackinder said the following: "Who rules East Europe commands the Heartland. Who rules the Heartland commands the World-Island. Who rules the World-Island commands the world."

This is precisely the policy which was advocated by Bernard Lewis, another Brit. It was advocated by National Security Advisor Zbigniew Brzezinski under President Carter. It led Lyndon LaRouche to produce the video, *Storm Over Asia*. Their whole idea was to create an Arc of Crisis surrounding the Soviet Union, at the time of Carter and Brzezinski, and later against the former Soviet Union. That's what we're dealing with right now with regime change policies.

The Russians and Chinese have posed a coherent alternative to that with the intervention in Syria, the proposal for collaboration to fight terrorism, and with China's adoption of the policy which Lyndon and Helga LaRouche have fought for for decades—the World Land-Bridge or the One Belt, One Road, which is a win-win policy, as opposed to a geopolitical policy. The British are committed to preventing this so-called Heartland from being developed. That British geopolitics is the policy that led to two world wars.

To Win the War—Understand Your Enemy

This is what we're up against. If the British are successful in the effort to impeach, carry out a coup against, or assassinate the President—we're heading toward a Third World War, which would be thermonuclear. That's the reality of the situation. That's what is at stake! A major part of the problem is the way in which the British have operated to control the way people think, including Americans, but not limited to Americans. For instance, Bertrand Russell was a key figure. Lyndon LaRouche has called him the most evil man of the 20th Century. This is a guy whom many regard as a peacenik, but who advocated carrying out nuclear strikes against the Soviet Union, before he knew they had nuclear weapons. But, more fundamentally, he pushed a philosophy that denied creativity, the actual source of scientific development and economic development. He put forward a mathematical form of thinking, and that's the way the British have always operated.

There are certain ideas which have become hegemonic in society and in academia, including the idea that the Universe is ruled by entropy, that the Universe is winding down, and there are limits to growth. And if you use up limited resources, there will be a catastrophe; therefore, we have to reduce population. We cannot industrialize because it will use up limited resources; and that man is the cause of climate change because he industrializes. This is the fundamental conception which is scientifically fraudulent, but has taken over.

You can look throughout history, where such ideas have been imposed, they're enforced. For instance, the

Elizabeth (foreground), now Queen, makes the Nazi salute.

idea that the Earth is flat, or the belief in Euclidian geometry, which is that linearity is primary as opposed to curvature, which is connected with the idea that the Earth is flat. During the whole era of the Middle Ages, it was believed that the Emperor in Europe derived his power from the Pope; it was a divine right, and the Pope determined who was the Holy Roman Emperor, and this was attributed to the "Donation of Constantine." But, as Nicholas of Cusa and Dante before him, and others, pointed out, this was a complete fraud. But you had to destroy that idea—an idea that everybody was afraid to challenge—in order to arrive at the actual reality, which is that the power to govern derives from the people: It has to be an informed people, it has to be a people who are acting intelligently, not just ultra-democracy, as in the democracy policies of regime change.

This was the British approach—to control the way in which people think, by reducing their thinking to mathematics, to what's called induction. You go from sense-perception to a conclusion which is actually derived from a fixed assumption. Take the chemical bombings. You see a video on television,—that's your sense-perception—an atrocity, a child was injured. It could have been completely staged and most likely was. But you see that, and then what happens? From a deductive standpoint: this is the Russians—it's always the Russians, or Assad, they demonize them. But where's the evidence? They never went to the scene, but people accept this kind of thing.

Or the so-called hack of the DNC computers: You're told from CrowdStrike—which is the company hired by the DNC, two of whose leading figures used to work at the FBI with Mueller (now the Special Counsel)—that this was the Russians. Then you are manipulated into this entire operation, which is destroying this country and the world. The urgent necessity is to break out of this kind of mental control, and recognize the actual nature of man is to be creative, not to just operate on the basis of induction and deduction. That's the philosophy of the British System, empiricism, the method of Francis Bacon, John Locke, all of these so-called philosophers who were just agents of the British Empire.

Always remember that the goal of the royal family, the Nazi-loving royal family, is to reduce the world's population from its current level to one billion—at most. That is real genocide. That's the policy of Zeus from Greek mythology, as opposed to the policy of Prometheus which was to develop mankind—to give science, give technology, give fire. That is the more fundamental issue that people have to actually think about—how they think—and not be afraid. You've got to actually break through this environment, which has been created, and mobilize. That is what we've got to do at this point: Mobilize to make sure that the truth comes out with respect to this whole issue of the so-called DNC hacking; mobilize to ensure that this sanctions bill is reversed. Even more importantly, mobilize for collaboration between the United States, Russia, and China, and potentially India, to dismantle the British Empire once and for all, before it destroys humanity. That is the fundamental issue before us right now.

There are economic policies which Lyndon LaRouche has outlined—the *Four Laws*—which are crucial. That's what has to move forward. That would move us into coherence with Russia and China, as opposed to these sanctions.

That is, I think, the crux of what I wanted to develop.

Every Day Counts In Today's Showdown To Save Civilization

NEW REDUCED PRICE!

That's why you need EIR's **Daily Alert Service**, a strategic overview compiled with the input of Lyndon LaRouche, and delivered to your email 5 days a week.

The election of Donald Trump to the Presidency of the Untied States has launched a new global era whose character has yet to be determined. The Obama-Clinton drive toward confrontation with Russia has been disrupted--but what will come next?

Over the next weeks and months there will be a pitched battle to determine the course of the Trump Administration. Will it pursue policies of cooperation with Russia and China in the New Silk Road, as the President-Elect has given some signs of? Will it follow through against Wall Street with Glass-Steagall?

The opposition to these policies will be fierce. If there is to be a positive outcome to this battle, an informed citizenry must do its part--intervening, educating, inspiring. That's why you need the EIR Daily Alert more than ever.

TUESDAY, NOVEMBER 22, 2016

Volume 3, Number 65

EIR Daily Alert Service

P.O. Box 17390, Washington, DC 20041-0390

- Only Global Solutions, Based on New Principles, Can Work
- Tulsi Gabbard Meets with Donald Trump Regarding Syria
- Robert Kagan Throws in the Towel, Complains U.S. Is Becoming 'Solipsistic'
- War Party Moving To Preempt Trump-Putin Reset
- Syrian Army Makes More Progress in Aleppo
- Duterte Gives OK to Nuclear Power for Philippines
- Europe Will Suffer from Maintaining Russia Sanctions
- Former Chilean Diplomat Confirmed, 'We Will Joyfully Welcome Xi Jinping'
- Duterte and Putin Establish Philippines-Russia Cooperation
- François Fillon, Pro-Russian Thatcherite, Wins First Round of French Right-Wing Presidential Primary

EDITORIAL

Only Global Solutions, Based on New Principles, Can Work

NOVEMBER 21, 1993

On LaRouche's Discovery

by Lyndon H. LaRouche, Jr.

The central feature of my original contribution to the Leibniz science of physical economy, is the provision of a method for addressing the causal relationship between, on the one side, individuals' contributions to axiomatically revolutionary advances in scientific and analogous forms of knowledge, and, on the other side, consequent increases in the *potential population-density* of corresponding societies. In its application to political economy, my method focuses analysis upon the central role of the following, three-step sequence: first, axiomatically revolutionary forms of scientific and analogous discovery; second, consequent advances in machine-tool and analogous principles; finally, consequent advances in the productive powers of labor.

These discoveries were initially the outgrowth of 1948-1952 objections to the inappropriateness of Norbert Wiener's application of statistical information theory to describing both the characteristic distinctions of living processes and of communication of ideas.[1] I countered with a contrary, non-statistical definition of negentropy, as that meaning of the term might be de-

rived from the common, physically distinguishing characteristic of an evolutionary biosphere. This non-statistical counter-definition of negentropy was then stated in terms of a successfully self-developing physical economy; the efficient impact of scientific discoveries' communication within such a negentropic physical-economic process was treated as most typical of the communication of ideas in general.

That was the initial core of my discovery, up to the year 1952. Yet, up to that point, the appropriate mathematical representation of such a form of physical-economic negentropy was still wanted. The third step, taken through an intensive 1952 study of Georg Cantor's 1897 *Beiträge*,[2] opened the doors of the transfinite domain upon a fresh insight into relevant features of Bernhard Riemann's contributions.[3] Thence, the applied form of my definition of physical-economic negentropy acquired the title of "LaRouche-Riemann Method."[4]

---

1. *Cf.* Norbert Wiener, *Cybernetics, or Control and Communication in the Animal and the Machine* (New York: John Wiley, 1948); 2nd ed., (Cambridge, Mass: M.I.T. Press, 1961).

Editors' Note: Readers of these footnotes should be aware that Lyndon LaRouche wrote this work in Federal pententiary, where he was unjustly incarcerated for five years after being framed up by George H.W. Bush. For that reason, most of the body of these footnotes was written by his associates, with varying degrees of guidance from Mr. LaRouche. But rather than try to re-establish now what LaRouche himself would have written, we have left them as they were published earlier, except for footnote 60, which has been replaced.

2. Georg Cantor, "Beiträge zur Begründung der transfiniten Mengenlehre," in *Georg Cantors Gesammelte Abhandlungen,* ed. by Ernst Zermelow (Hildesheim, 1962), pp. 282-356; English translation: *Contributions to the Founding of the Theory of Transfinite Numbers,* trans. by Philip E.B. Jourdain (1915) (New York: Dover Publications, 1941).
3. Bernhard Riemann, "Über die Hypothesen welche der Geometrie zu Grunde liegen," in *Mathematische Werke,* 2nd ed. (1892), ed. by Heinrich Weber in collaboration with R. Dedekind. English translation: "On the Hypotheses Which Lie at the Foundations of Geometry," in David Eugene Smith, *A Source Book in Mathematics* (New York: Dover Publications, 1959), pp. 411-425.
4. From late 1979 to the close of 1983, the international newsweekly *Executive Intelligence Review* produced a quarterly economic forecast based upon the *LaRouche-Riemann method.* This report was constructed quarterly from, primarily, a GNP-defined data-base, using a set of constraints supplied by this author. During this period, that was the only consistently reliable published forecast available from any U.S. source. This forecasting was discontinued during early 1988, at this author's recommendation. The margin of fakery in U.S. government and

I. Negentropy in Physical Economy

Initially, during 1948-1952, I made two principal arguments against Norbert Wiener's application of statistical method to living processes. The first of these two was, that, insofar as we employ the term "negative entropy" to signify the characteristic distinction of living processes in general, the phenomenon referenced cannot be described either in terms of a simple time-reversal of thermodynamical statistical entropy, or in terms of the term "energy" used as a notion reducible to a scalar measure of heat. The second of the two objections was, that, for similar, related reasons, statistical information theory has no appropriate application to the processes of generation and communication of ideas.

On the first of these two classes of objections, the kernel of the matter is, that, for the case of an indefinitely successfully self-developing biosphere, the imputable ratio of free energy to energy of the system increases at the same time that the total energy of the system increases, and, that, similarly and concurrently, the ratio of free energy to rising energy-flux density is also rising.

The second of the two objections is brought to light more conveniently, by examining the analogous case of a successfully evolving physical economy. The obviously intrinsic advantage of this choice of subject-matter is that metrical characteristics of the phenomena are predefined in the clearest way: input-output relations of physical labor and physical consumption, defined in *per capita* and *per* square-kilometer measures. The most readily accessible illustration of this argument is provided, broadly, by successful models of modern, post-fourteenth-century economies of the type addressed by Leibniz's 1672-1716 work of founding that science of physical economy also known as the science of technology.[5] Such cases are typified by the characteristic feature of generally increasing intensity of use of heat-powered machinery. The measurement of such model cases in terms of both *per capita* and *per* square-kilometer caloric values of input and output, leads to an array of inequality relationships, by means of which the most relevant relations can be measured comparatively in terms of chronological successions of changes of state of each such economy studied as an integrated whole process.

Only the evolutionary model of such a heat- powered process of increase of the productive powers of labor brings the meaningful issues into focus. By contrast, any zero-growth, non-evolutionary model of physical economy is axiomatically entropic, and corresponds to no durably successful model of national or global economy.

For the evolutionary case, progress in scientific and analogous forms of knowledge is the driver of those changes in practice which lead toward a consequent expression of the indicated, life-like negentropic forms of economic development. It should be stressed, that this role of generation and communication of ideas is illustrated by considering Leibniz's study of the proposals for an industrial development based upon the combination of heat-powered machinery and analogous thermodynamical development of modes of production and transport generally. This Leibniz case is a bench-mark from which the history of physical economy in general may be traced backward and forward in time.

That Leibniz case, of increase of the productive powers of labor through employment of the heat-powered machine, has two readily identified, ironically juxtaposed aspects. First, immediately, there is the simpler aspect, the increase of productive powers of labor, in some functional correlation with increase of heat power supplied efficiently *per capita* and *per* square kilometer. In the complementary aspect, on account of nothing other than some improvement in employed principles of design, one machine, using no more power than a comparable second machine, yields greater increase of the productive powers of labor. The second case, the general notion of an efficient improvement in design principle, illustrates the notion of *technology*.

For purposes of analysis, the term technology must denote a set of all those machine-tool and analogous principles of design which may be derived commonly from, implicitly subsumed by a specific, axiomatically unique quality of scientific or analogous discovery. Reference the refined design of a crucial experiment employed to demonstrate the proof of principle of a

---

Federal Reserve System data rendered any report using such data worthless. See "Riemannian analysis predicts industrial top shutdown," *Executive Intelligence Review,* Vol. VI, No. 41, Oct. 23-29, 1979; and " 'Spectral Analysis' of Collapse," *New Solidarity,* Vol. X, No. 71, Nov. 9, 1979, p. 8.

5. See G.W. Leibniz, "On the Establishment of a Society in Germany for the Promotion of the Arts and Sciences" (1671) and "Society and Economy" (1671), *Fidelio,* Vol. I, No. 2, Spring 1992 and Vol. I, No. 3, Fall 1992.

crucial scientific hypothesis. Each type of such refined experimental design for that same crucial hypothesis subsumes a set of machine-tool principles, or a *technology*; all of the sets subsumed by crucial proof-of-principle design for that same hypothesis constitute a family of such sets, or a family of *technologies* derived from that proof of principle.

Thus, does scientific discovery lead, typically, through subsumed technologies, toward consequent increases in the productive powers of labor. The relevant task of analysis in physical economy is to show that such generation and transmission of valid creative discoveries, as ideas, is the source of the realized negentropy of physical economies, and, hence, of negentropic increases of the potential population-density of mankind in our universe. My argument, in opposition to statistical information theory, was, that the generation and transmission of such noetic (negentropic) ideas exhibits fundamentally the principle underlying, bounding externally, the transmission of ideas in general.

This discovery posed two paradoxes. The first of these paradoxes is the formal difficulties posed by stating that the characteristic of all physical-economic processes which meet persistently the standard of increasing potential population-density, is negentropy. The apparent paradox lies in the fact that I defined negentropy as corresponding to an increase of the ratio of free energy to energy, and to energy-density of the system, under the condition that the energy of the system is continually increasing both *per capita* and *per* square kilometer.

The second of these two paradoxes is the notion of the functional role of technology's mathematical discontinuities in the theory of heat-powered machinery.

Perhaps it may be said, that, as treasures of pagan mythology are guarded by dragons, forbidding paradoxes often deter the timid from reaching out to the crucial discoveries otherwise within their reach. These apparent paradoxes of my argument proved not the weakness, but rather precisely the strength of my case against positivists such as Wiener, John Von Neumann[6] *et al.*

II. The Paradoxes of Negentropy

To define my post-1951 attack upon the metrical problem, consider the following.

The two paradoxes identified above should be recognized as echoing the issue of Isaac Newton's confession as to the source of his so-called "Clockwinder" paradox. Newton warned, thus, that the false-to-nature image of an entropic universe had infected his *Principia* through defects inhering in what he regarded as his only available choice of mathematics.[7] But for my adolescent grounding in such relevant works as the *Clark-Leibniz Correspondence*[8] and *Monadology*,[9] I, too, would probably have been frightened off the track of my discovery by the appearance of the indicated paradoxes.

The influence of Leibniz upon my view of these two paradoxes is situated historically, summarily, as follows.

In synopsis, the relevant background of Newton's *"Clock-winder" problem"* is this. Although the solar-astronomy roots of modern mathematical science reach back far beyond 6,000 B.C. in Vedic Central Asia[10] and

---

7. Sir Isaac Newton states in his famous four theological letters to the Reverend Dr. Richard Bentley: "That gravity should be innate, inherent, and essential to matter, so that one body may act upon another at a distance through a *vacuum,* without the mediation of anything else, by and through which their action and force may be conveyed from one to another, is to me so great an absurdity that I believe no man who has in philosophical matters a competent faculty of thinking can ever fall into it. Gravity must be caused by an agent acting constantly according to certain laws, but whether this agent be material or immaterial I have left to the consideration of my readers. . . ."; cited in *Newton's Philosophy of Nature: Selections From His Writings,* ed. by H.S. Thayer (New York: Hafner Press, 1953), pp. 54-57. See also Samuel Clarke's defense of Newton in "The Controversy between Leibniz and Clarke," footnote 8 below, p. 1104. This point is alluded to by Newton in both the General Scholium to his *Principia* (*Mathematical Principles of Natural Philosophy*), and in the concluding Quest. 31 (Book Three, Part I) of his *Opticks.*
8. See Gottfried Wilhelm Leibniz, "The Controversy between Leibniz and Clarke," in *Gottfried Wilhelm Leibniz Philosophical Papers and Letters*, ed. by Leroy E. Loemker (Chicago: University of Chicago Press, 1956), vol. II, pp. 1095-1169.
9. See Gottfried Wilhelm Leibniz, *Monadology,* trans. by George Montgomery (LaSalle: Open Court Publishing Co., 1989).
10. See Lokamanya Bal Gangadhar Tilak, *The Orion; Or, Researches into the Antiquity of the Vedas* (1893), 5th ed. (Poona: Shri J.S. Tilak, Tilak Bros., 1972), and *The Arctic Home in the Vedas, Being Also a New Key to the Interpretation of Many Vedic Texts and Legends* (1903) (Poona: Tilak Bros., 1956). Astronomical observations recorded in certain amongst the ancient Vedic hymns place their date of composition at an outside limit of approximately 6,000-4,000 B.C. (*The Orion*); more

---

6. For John Von Neumann's initial proposal to simulate economics and other "social phenomena" by sets of linear inequalities, see "Zur Theorie der Gesellschaftsspiele," *Math. Ann.* 100, 1928, pp. 295-320), reprinted in *John Von Neumann: Collected Works* (New York: Pergamon Press, 1963), Vol. V, pp. 1-26. See also, John Von Neumann and Oscar Morgenstern, *The Theory of Games and Economic Behavior* (Princeton, N.J.: Princeton University Press, 1944); and Von Neumann's posthumously published *The Computer and the Brain (Silliman Lectures)* (New Haven: Yale University Press, 1958).

in the culture of China,[11] a comprehensive, mathematical basis for a unified body of science ("natural philosophy") was first founded by Nicolaus of Cusa, *et al.* during the early middle decades of Europe's fifteenth-century Golden Renaissance of Cusa, Piccolomini, Toscanelli, Leonardo da Vinci, Raphael, *et al.*[12] The complication, leading to Newton's "Clockwinder" problem, was the spread of a Venice-directed opposition to the Council of Florence, an attack which featured the neo-Aristotelian empiricism of such Gasparo Contarini associates as Pomponazzi[13] and the Franciscan cabalist Francesco Zorzi.[14] Through this continuing influence upon England of such Venetian potencies as the notorious Paolo Sarpi, we have Baconian empiricism and British philosophical liberalism generally.

Respecting the two paradoxes originally posed to me by my theses against statistical information theory, the relevant problems in mathematics are a tangle of two respectively distinct, but interlocked sets of problems. Once this tangle is understood from an historical vantage-point, my solution to the cited paradoxes is more readily intelligible.

The founding work of modern science is Nicolaus of Cusa's *De Docta Ignorantia,*[15] in which the pivotal mathematical discovery referenced is Nicolaus' revolutionary treatment of Archimedes' theorems on quadrature of the circle.[16] Nicolaus' new solution for these theorems[17] is also a form of demonstration of the general solution for the ontological paradox depicted within Plato's *Parmenides* dialogue.[18] Nicolaus's discovery is, in fact, an illustration of Plato's principle of human knowledge: *hypothesizing the higher hypothesis.*[19]

To this, the anti-Renaissance associates of Gasparo Contarini counterposed, violently, the dogma of *neo-Aristotelian empiricism,* the deductive treatment of sense-certainty, which is otherwise recognizable as the philosophical "materialism" of the Renaissance's seventeenth and eighteenth centuries' principal adversary, the Enlightenment. Thus the spread of the Enlighten-

---

speculative indications of earlier, Arctic astronomical observations in these sources, would push back fragments of these hymns to the period no later than the climate shift accompanying the ending of the last Ice Age (*Arctic Home*).

11. The British holist biologist Joseph Needham, whose encyclopedic writings on the history of science and technology in China dominate twentieth-century scholarship, went to great lengths to discredit or cover up the discoveries made in the nineteenth century concerning ancient Chinese astronomy. The French scientist Edouard Biot and the Dutch philologist Gustav Schlegel, proved from evidence in the Confucian classics that astronomical science was already highly developed in the third millennium **b.c.**; and Schlegel's research led him to hypothesize that significant mapping of the heavens existed at the extremely early date of the sixteenth millennium **b.c.** Needham, while acknowledging the authority and competence of these scientists, labeled their findings as "quite absurd" and "purely legendary," lying that they had little support and that they "served to discredit what real historical research might reveal"—this because, in keeping with British historiography, Needham insisted such knowledge had necessarily to be "derived from Babylonian sources." See Joseph Needham, *Science and Civilization in China* (London: Cambridge University Press, 1954), Vol. III; Edouard Biot, *Le Tcheou-Li: ou, Rites des Tcheou,* traduit pour le premier fois du chinois par feu Edouard Biot (Paris: 1851) (Taipei: Ch'eng Wen Publishing Co., 1969); Gustav Schlegel and Dr. Franz Künert, *Shu King Finsterniss,* Journal V.K.A.W.A.-L, Amsterdam, 1890; Gustav Schlegel, *Uranograthie Chinoise* (Leyden and The Hague: 1875).

12. The Golden Renaissance of the fifteenth century is centered around the 1439-1440 Council of Florence as the principal event. Nicolaus of Cusa is the principal figure of that period, whose work on science directly shaped the work of such figures as Leonardo da Vinci and Luca Pacioli and indirectly thus the entire school of Raphael and also the work of Kepler.

13. Pietro Pomponazzi (1462-1525); philosopher who enjoyed the patronage of the Contarini family, he studied and taught at the University of Padua. Pomponazzi took Averroës as his point of departure, and by dichotomizing discourse into the philosophical and the religious, argued that according to reason the soul must die with the body, but according to the teaching of Christianity, we know it to be immortal; this argument appears in his major work, *De Immortalitate Animae* (On the Immortality of Souls) (Bologna: 1516). See *The Renaissance Philosophy of Man,* ed. by Ernst Cassirer, Paul O. Kristeller, and J.H. Randall (Chicago: University of Chicago Press, 1948); also see *Studi su Pietro Pomponazzi* ed. by B. Nardi (Florence, 1965).

14. Francesco Zorzi (or Giorgi), a Franciscan friar descended from the patrician Zorzi family of Venice. Authored *De Harmonia Mundi* (1525), a mystical work with elements deriving from the Cabbala. Zorzi supported the arguments of King Henry VIII of England when Henry sought the annulment of his marriage to Catherine of Aragon, and he was called to the English royal court, where he remained active between 1531 and his death in 1540. Zorzi was a proponent of a satanic and pseudo-Platonic school of mysticism called Rosicrucianism, which became an important component of English and British Freemasonry.

15. See Nicolaus of Cusa, *De Docta Ignorantia (On Learned Ignorance),* trans. by Jasper Hopkins as *Nicholas of Cusa on Learned Ignorance* (Minneapolis: Arthur M. Banning Press, 1985).

16. *Ibid.,* Book I, chap. 3, pp. 52-53.

17. See Nicolaus of Cusa, "De Circuli Quadratura" ("On the Quadrature of the Circle"), German trans. by Jay Hoffman (Mainz: Felix Meiner Verlag); see English trans. by William F. Wertz, Jr., in *Fidelio,* Vol. 3, No.1, Spring 1994, p.56-63.

18. As noted in the text below, there is a precise equivalence as to method between the *Parmenides* dialogue of Plato and the method employed by Nicolaus of Cusa to make his discovery in connection with his reading and reconstruction of Archimedes' treatment of quadrature.

19. See the celebrated image of the Divided Line in Plato's *Republic,* in *Plato: The Republic,* Loeb Classical Library, trans. by Paul Shorey (Cambridge: Harvard University Press), vol. II, Steph. pp. 507a-511e, esp. pp. 510a-e.

ment's cabalistic empiricism is typified by the influence of such notables as Francis Bacon, Robert Fludd, Elias Ashmole, René Descartes, Isaac Newton, John Locke, and Immanuel Kant.

The view of the problem of quadrature from the standpoint of Plato's *Parmenides* shows, perhaps most efficiently, the root of Newton's "Clockwinder" failure, and exposes also the more general form of practical differences in scientific results between the two opposed, Renaissance and Enlightenment, methods of work. This shows explicitly, in this way, the implication of my initial treatment of my own two scientific paradoxes.

The gist of the matter is as follows.

The Archimedean quadrature of the circle relies upon the so-called method of exhaustion famously employed by Plato's collaborator, Eudoxus. By simultaneously inscribing and circumscribing regular polygons, of the same species, and by increasing the number of sides of these polygons, equally and concurrently, we may estimate the value of π accurately to any desired decimal place. Slovenly thinking would argue, mistakenly, from this, that the perimeters of the two polygons must ultimately coincide with a circular perimeter.[20]

The same species of philosophical problem arises in deriving the uniqueness of the five Platonic solids. In the case of quadrature, what exhaustion proves, is that, never, even at conjectural infinity, could the number of sides be increased sufficiently to produce coincidence of the polygonal and circular perimeters. Thus is illustrated by the fact that a circle, as a species, is not constructible by a geometry premised hereditarily upon the axiomatic assumption of self-evident point and straight line; another, axiomatically different geometry must be adopted, one in which circular action supplants axiomatic definition of point and straight line.

Two points representing the case are relevant for understanding my solution to the negentropy paradoxes.

First, very briefly, the fact that point and straight line are theorem-existences in a geometry premised upon circular action, but not the reverse, shows that the noncircular forms externally (epistemologically) bounded by circular action (in this sense of external bounding) have only that inferior, dependent existence, dependent upon the necessary existence of the higher. This, notably, is an argument congruent with the ontological

proof of existence of God. Thus, the mind must, so to speak, leap from the falsely imagined elementary of the simpler, to recognize that the elementary lies actually in the superior. Thus, does human reason free man from subjugation to the bestiality of neo-Aristotelian sense-certainty. This appearance of an ontological leap typifies the phenomenal guise of creative thought.

This is the same species of problem posed by Plato's *Parmenides,* that problem, which, as paradox, blocks the pathway to that true knowledge, which is opposite to mere sense-certainty, derived uniquely, not from simple deductive sense-certainty; this true knowledge is typified by the recognition that a necessary existent, which bounds externally a set of phenomena of mere sense-certainty, is the relative ontological reality, the relative One, which adumbrates the mere shadow-existence of sensory appearances.

Thus, Cusa's treatment of quadrature implicitly defined ("hereditarily") the non-algebraic higher mathematics which Leibniz and Johann Bernoulli proved physically by the case of light refraction, a quarter-millennium later.[21] This gave modern science two levels of mathematics, the lower, the algebraic, and the higher, the non-algebraic, the latter later called transcendental.

Second, still later, by the same method of discovery employed in Plato's *Parmenides,* and used by Cusa in his treatment of Archimedean quadrature, Georg Cantor, two hundred years after Jean Bernoulli's announcement,[22] announced the discovery of a third, still higher domain of mathematics, the transfinite, superseding the transcendental.[23] It is only a view of the relatively subsumed, transcendental, space-time continuum, a view obtained from the standpoint of the transfinite, which permits an adequate comprehension of cognitive problems underlying the deductively apparent paradoxes of negentropy.

By 1951, the specific, narrowly defined difficulty which confronted me was, that any function defined in terms of those successive, axiomatic transformations which correspond to generalized, continuing scientific-

---

20. See Lyndon H. LaRouche, Jr., "On the Subject of Metaphor," *Fidelio,* Vol. I, No. 3, Fall 1992, pp. 18-20; see also, Nicolaus of Cusa, "De Circuli Quadratura," *op. cit.*

21. See Johann Bernoulli, "Curvatura radii in diaphanis nonuniformibus…" ("The curvature of a ray in nonuniform media, and the solution of the problem to find the brachistochrone, that is, the curve on which a heavy point falls from a given position to another given position in the shortest time, as well as the construction of the synchrone or the wave of the rays"), *Acta Eruditorum,* May 1697; trans. in D.J. Struik, *A Source Book in Mathematics, 1200-1800* (Princeton, N.J.: Princeton University Press, 1986), pp. 391-396.

22. *Ibid.*

23. Georg Cantor, *Beiträge, op. cit.*

technological progress, cannot be represented functionally by any generally accepted form of classroom mathematics. I view that as a more general form of the difficulty which trapped a misled Newton into an entropic, "Clock-winder" morass.

I expressed my own notion of negentropy in such paradoxical terms which posed that conception most simply. To this purpose, I adopted conditionally the implicit assumption of customary, classroom algebraic physics, that any body of algebraically formal scientific knowledge, up to the moment of an axiomatic-revolutionary advancement of principle, is being perfected formally as a consistent, deductive theorem-lattice. In that case, the arrival of the axiomatic-revolutionary discovery represents, deductively, an absolute mathematical discontinuity separating axiomatically knowledge preceding the discovery from that which follows. So, the formal representation of a function corresponding to a succession of such axiomatic discoveries is depicted essentially as a function in terms of what appeared to deductive formalism as absolute mathematical discontinuities.

It follows, that if the discoveries of that succession each represent implicitly an increase of the productive powers of labor, the historically cumulative density of the formal discontinuities so portrayed represents an increasing *power* of knowledge. This notion of power of a so-selected succession of formal discontinuities, describes the needed alternative to ordinary classroom notions of function. Such is the functional form of this alternative definition of both biological and physical-economic negentropy.

My 1952 study of Cantor's *Beiträge* provided the key to developing this conception further. Following that study, later the same year, I was electrified by re-reading the relevant, most crucial passage of Riemann's habilitation dissertation.[24] Applying the Cantorian implications of my own notion of negentropy to Riemann's stated crucial problem of a continuous manifold "sent sparks flying in all directions." Cantor's transfinite was key to bringing the two elements together in this way, my own and Riemann's.

This combined view of the universe of physical economy's experience, seen as a functional continuum, guided me to construct revisions in the applicable theory of knowledge: to exclude all residues of sense-certainty's notion of linear ontological elementarity, and to replace these entirely by the elementarity of universal, negentropically evolutionary *change,* in Heraclitus' and Plato's sense of the ontological elementarity of nothing but change.

This required that the popular idea of a mathematical certainty must be put aside, to be superseded by a corrected view of the theory of knowledge. No system of deductive contemplation of our sense-experience can be human knowledge; we know the universe only to the degree we surpass sense-certainty by reflection upon the willful means through which we increase man's power over our universe.

This aspect of mankind's relationship to nature is the central feature of the Leibniz science of physical economy. All matters are subject to crucial tests in terms of choices of pathway of scientific changes in axioms, pathways which generate successive increases in mankind's potential population-density, as the latter relationship to our universe is measured relative to our planet Earth.[25]

I argued that this physical-economic definition of knowledge implicitly defines a superior scientific method, and, therefore, a fresh overview of the term "mathematics" from a higher standpoint.

In recent decades, I have underscored the following, subsidiary form of that latter argument. I argue that what these reflections pose for mathematics is typified by the ontological paradox of method central to Plato's *Parmenides.* That dialogue is to be recognized, taken together with Cusa's treatment of quadrature for this purpose, as a forerunner of Cantor's conception of the transfinite, and also as a precedent for Kurt Gödel's derived, comprehensive refutation of the radical positivist fallacies permeating axiomatically the central mathematical theses of Betrand Russell, John Von Neumann, and other beliefs of that positivist genre, including Wiener's information theory.[26]

---

24. Bernhard Riemann, "On the Hypotheses Which Lie at the Foundations of Geometry," *op. cit.,* pp. 422-425.

25. This view of potential population-density connotes a higher definition of our human species: first, as man in our solar system, and, next, as galactic man yearning toward a universal mankind.

26. See Kurt Gödel's "Richardian paradox," in Kurt Gödel, *On Formally Undecidable Propositions of* Principia Mathematica *and Related Systems,* (New York: Dover, 1992); also "The Consistency of the Axiom of Choice and of the Generalized Continuum Hypothesis," *Proceedings of the National Association of Science U.S.A.,* 24 (1938), pp. 556-557. See also Ernest Nagel and James R. Newman, *Gödel's Proof* (New York: New York University Press, 1958), pps. 60-63, 66, 85-86. Gödel directly refuted Von Neumann's "finitist approach" approach in a letter published in *The Theory of Self-Reproducing Automata,* by John Von

Typical of this ontological implication of the *Parmenides* is Cusa's discovery, that the circle does not come into existence, "even at infinity," by means of any merely formal geometry of the axiomatically rectilinear theorem-lattice kind. As an outcome of that discovery by Cusa, *circular action,* also known (later) as Leibnizian *least action,* is recognized *ontologically* as an independently higher form of existence, an existence which bounds externally all merely algebraic space-time.

From this argument, it follows, that the term "reason" must not be used as Kant does, must not be degraded to a mere synonym of mechanistic, linear "logic." Reason must signify, typically, valid modes of those kinds of axiomatically-revolutionary discovery, modes by means of which ontologically higher forms of existence, such as Cusa's circular action, are shown to be the necessary existence bounding externally an array of inferior, predicated phenomena. Hence, the recommended use of the descriptive term "creative reason," to place the needed emphasis upon this intelligible use of the terms "creative" and "reason."

Such is the principle of creative reason demonstrated by Cusa's treatment of quadrature. One should return to this application of Plato's *Parmenides* by Cusa, to illustrate the proper, constructive-geometrical standpoint from which to comprehend the ontological implications of Cantor's superseding of transcendental, merely mathematical, merely symbolic space-time, by the higher ontological standpoint of transfinite *physical space-time.*

It must be recognized, in this way, that the successive levels of mathematics—algebraic, Leibnizian non-algebraic (transcendental), transfinite—define a transfinite array of predicates of a shared common *type.*[27] All three of these are each traceable directly from Cusa's treatment of Archimedean quadrature.[28] Each is separated formally from its predecessor by an axiomatic-revolutionary change, a true mathematical discontinuity (singularity). Each change is effected in an equivalent way, referenced to a common point of origin; and, thus, the array qualifies as a *type.* Each change illustrates the Platonic principle of *hypothesis*; the array as a *type* illustrates the Platonic principle of *higher hypothesis.* That array of successively higher *types* which is physical scientific (as distinct from merely mathematical) progress, is a higher *type* of a transfinitely ordered array of higher hypotheses: in other words, a *higher type,* corresponding to Plato's notion of hypothesizing the higher hypothesis.

Thus, Cantor's discovery of that transfinite which bounds externally the mathematically transcendental, might appear to be the solution for the mathematical appearance of a paradox in my definition of negentropy. Certainly, this was an indispensable step, but did not represent a complete solution of that paradox. Negentropy is essentially a notion of causality; mathematics, even a merely mathematical notion of the transfinite, is not a true physics, but only a higher form of symbolism; such mathematics cannot represent causality as such. Another step was required. A turn to Riemann's work, later during 1952, pointed the direction to the needed next step.

III. Negentropy as 'Ontologically Transfinite'

Situate Riemann's significance for my work, by restating briefly the context for the 1952 reading of, especially, Riemann's *Hypothesen.*

From 1948 on, through 1951, my anti-reductionist notion of negentropy was developed into approximately the form it may be broadly described today. Yet, until my "electrified" reactions to successive, 1952 studies in the work of Cantor and Riemann, it remained unclear to me how to situate this seemingly paradoxical conception with respect to generally accepted forms of classroom mathematical physics.

The geometrical solution to this paradox was supplied, in large part, by aid of Cantor's *Beiträge,* but only with respect to mathematical formalities. As already stated, *mathematics as such cannot represent causality,*

Neumann, edited and completed by Arthur W. Burks (Urbana and London: University of Illinois Press, 1966), pp. 53-59. Gödel points out in this letter to Burks that Von Neumann's approach is "in line with the finitistic way of thinking," like that of Alan Turing. In remarks published postumously in *Kurt Gödel: Collected Works* (New York: Oxford University Press, 1990), Vol. II ("Some remarks on the undecidability results 1972a" and "A philosophical error in Turing's work"), Gödel states that "Turing in his 1937, p. 250 (1965, p. 136), gives an argument which is supposed to show that mental procedures cannot go beyond mechanical procedures. However, this argument is inconclusive. What Turing disregards completely is the fact that *mind, in its use, is not static, but constantly developing. . . .*" See footnote 6 for relevant works of Von Neumann.

27. For *type,* see Georg Cantor, "Beiträge," *op. cit.*

28. Nicolaus of Cusa, "De Circuli Quadratura," *op. cit.*

and the central feature of my notion of negentropy is causality as the elementarity of physical space-time. An ensuing study of relevant features of Riemann's arguments respecting the metrical qualities of a continuous manifold, prompted a conceptual insight into this remaining difficulty.

The explicit solution to the remaining margin of paradox is not to be found within those writings of Riemann which were published during his lifetime.[29] The relevant, electrifying, crucial passage from the habilitation dissertation had produced its needed effect only because two leading notions from the history of science were brought to bear upon that 1952 re-reading. The first of those two was the Heraclitus-Plato concept of the unique, universal, physical elementarity of change.[30] Re-read Riemann's crucial passage to the effect that the continuity of negentropy, as elementary change, is the ontological *type,* or *characteristic,* which defines a continuous manifold as continuous. The second of these two is Leibniz's 1714 *Monadology.* For emphasis, read that *Monadology* as it was incompetently attacked by Leonhard Euler.[31] On this latter account, regard Cantor's transfinite in its aspect as a devastating refutation of Euler's blunder, and, thus, a definitive, formal rehabilitation of Leibniz's *Monadology.*

Viewing my 1952 reading of the Riemann *Hypothesen* more broadly, five crucial conceptions were thus conjoined by this treatment of Riemann's uniquely relevant argument. *First,* the Heraclitus-Plato notion of the unique physical (i.e., causal) elementarity of *nothing but* change. *Second,* Leibniz's *monads. Third,* the Cantor mathematical transfinite. *Fourth,* my notion of negentropy. *Finally,* Riemann's treatment of the metrical paradoxes of a continuous manifold. If one substitutes for the materialist's fantastic, discrete elementarities of sense-perception-like objects, the Leibnizian sovereignty of existence of the individual monad, and if one were to show necessary and sufficient reason that a continuum, premised uniquely upon an elementary ontological quality of negentropic change, must necessar-

ily develop such efficient monads, the paradox, as paradox, were implicitly resolved.

That proof of the existence of monads which will be shown here, as I developed it, is provided from the combined standpoint of both the theory of knowledge and physical economy. An intervening, preparatory report must be provided at this point: assuming that negentropy of the relevant form does exist, what are the elementary mathematical implications of the existence of such a phenomenon?

From the standpoint of a *discrete manifold,* the discontinuity which is typical of a negentropic "power" function occupies a space-time location within the transcendental manifold *analogous to* the *transinfinitesimal* difference between an indefinitely extended algebraic quadrature and never-obtainable congruence with the relevant circular perimeter. It represents thus a Dedekind-like "cut," an interruption in the continuity of any otherwise apparently continuous line of the maximum of transcendental density of *denumerable* locations. It appears in merely mathematical space-time as an otherwise empty location of virtually-zero, virtually null-dimensional scale.

This is analogous to proposing for physics, that the discreteness of any sub-atomic, ostensibly elementary particle consists only of the virtually null-dimensional, mathematically circumscribed singularity embedded within a functional notion of that volume of merely mathematical space-time which the particle, as a phenomenon, is estimated to occupy.

The portent of this, is that the non-algebraic (transcendental) mathematical domain defines the location of phenomena in space-time. It cannot represent causality as such. It can pin-point the space-time "location of matter" with virtually inexhaustible refinement, but it does not define physical existence in any other sense than that of space-time location. As useful, even indispensable as this may be, it does not define a *physical space-time,* the latter the higher domain within which causality is expressed.

It is thus indicated, that we must not confuse the two mutually distinct ontological states, mere space-time and physical space-time. We must think of the *transcendental* as a certain image of space-time, a subsumed phase-space of the higher, externally bounding, *transfinite* domain of *physical space-time.*

Such reflections should prompt a reflection upon the character of those Cantor writings, notably his *Grundlagen* and *Mitteilungen,* which preceded his *Beiträge.* The *Beiträge* unveils the formal discovery of the trans-

---

29. See Bernhard Riemann, "Zur Psychologie und Metaphysik," on Herbart's Göttingen lectures, in *Mathematische Werke,* posthumous papers, *op. cit.*

30. As cited by Plato in *Cratylus,* in *Plato: Cratylus, Parmenides, Greater Hippias, Lesser Hippias,* trans. by H.N. Fowler, Steph. 402a; for Heraclitus, see G.S. Kirk and J.E. Raven, *The Presocratic Philosophers,* pp. 184-187, 197-198.

31. See Lyndon H. LaRouche, Jr., "Project A," Appendix XI, "Euler's Fallacies on the Subjects of Infinite Divisibility and Leibniz's Monads," in *The Science of Christian Economy and Other Prison Writings* (Washington, D.C.: Schiller Institute, 1991), pp. 407-425.

finite; the preceding writings, especially those cited two predecessors, enable us to recognize the process of Cantor's thinking, grounded, from the outset, in Karl Weierstrass's treatment of some of the demonstrable boundaries of Fourier analysis.[32] Cantor's extensive review of both ancient and modern philosophy[33] is an integral part of his preparations for developing the concept of the transfinite. As Cantor stresses the implications of his proof, that a higher-order mathematics, the transfinite, bounds externally the transcendental, space-time domain, require us to adopt afresh Plato's theory of knowledge. Specifically, Cantor's *transfinite* domain corresponds precisely to the intent of *Becoming* in Plato's theory of knowledge, as Cantor himself insists; similarly, the *Absolute,* which bounds demonstrably the transfinite, corresponds ontologically to that *Good* which bounds externally Plato's *Becoming.*[34]

This view of the Cantor to Plato parallels is not an optional topic in mathematics today. The central structural feature of the organization of the transfinite domain as a whole is Plato's theory of knowledge: *hypothesis, higher hypothesis,* and *hypothesizing the higher hypothesis.*[35] Cantor's notion of *type* and *equivalence* are cognate with that threefold structure of Plato's theory of knowledge.[36]

Cantor's emphasis upon the Classical philosophical theory of knowledge was in no sense gratuitous or even dispensable. Like the Cantor of my 1952 studies, I faced the requirement for a kind of proof which cannot be supplied merely by any localized sort of laboratory experiment. The appropriate experiment can be conducted only in the domain of physical economy in general. One must re-pose the Classical theory of knowledge as a study of the science of physical economy from the vantage-point of the study of the internal history of fundamental ("axiomatic") discoveries of higher principle within physical science in general. One must then prove whatever is adduced from the study in respect to progress in principles of composition in the Classical forms of plastic and non-plastic arts.[37] This proof, or its reflections, therefore occupies a leading place in my writings on political-economy or policy-shaping in general.[38]

The characteristic, absolute superiority of our human race over all lower species, is expressed implicitly by mankind's rise from a bestial, baboon-like, rock-artist-like potential population density of circa ten millions living individuals, to a technologically-determined potential of more than twenty-five billions today. This change is owed entirely to a quality which the Christian's Latin terms *imago Dei* and *capax Dei,* the Mosaic tradition of Genesis 1, that man, male and female alike, is cast in the image of God. This likeness is by virtue of that power of *creative reason* which is most simply illustrated by a revolutionary-axiomatic superseding of inferior by superior principle of scientific practice.[39] Thus, in effect, mankind is the only super-species, the only species which can willfully self-develop itself to the physical-economic equivalent of a succession of successively higher species.

To state this pivotal point very briefly, this quality of being such a "super-species" of creative reason is the image of negentropy as far as the human mind is capable of defining that notion. As such a "super-species," insofar as our physical-economic practice is premised upon such a continuing process of science-driven increase of our power of physical-economic practice, *per capita* and *per* square kilometer of our earth's habitable surface,[40] our conscious reflection upon our revolutionary practice is this idea of negentropy, this notion of the ontologically transfinite. This identifies a Platonic conceptualization of that ontological reality which adumbrates the mathematical imagery of Cantor's *Beiträge.*

32. See Georg Cantor, "Über trigonometrische Reihen," in *Gesammelte Abhandlungen mathematischen und philosophischen Inhalts,* ed. by E. Zermelo (Berlin: J. Springer, 1932; reprinted Hildesheim: Olms, 1966).

33. Here, "modern" signifies the period of Western European civilization beginning approximately A.D. 1400. This style emphasizes that both modern science and the modern form of nation-state republic were founded during the fifteenth century, both as leading, interdependent features of Europe's recovery from the rubble of the fourteenth-century "New Dark Age."

34. See, e.g., Plato's *Republic, op., cit.,* Steph. pp. 505a-520e.

35. See footnote 19.

36. *Ibid.* It is most relevant to note that this Platonic theory of knowledge permeates the philosophy of Plato-student Leibniz, his *Monadology* emphatically; this *monad* also appears under the rubric of *Geistesmassen* in Bernhard Riemann's posthumously published notes on Herbart's Göttingen lectures (see footnote 29).

37. For example, in 1952 this author first described the Classical *lied*'s interface between music and poetry as a "Rosetta Stone," in connection with a project refuting Norbert Wiener *et al.* on "information theory." See Lyndon H. LaRouche, Jr., "History As Science: America 2000," *Fidelio,* Vol. II, No. 3, Fall 1993, p. 32ff.

38. See Lyndon H. LaRouche, Jr.,"The Science of Christian Economy," in *Christian Economy, op. cit.,* pp. 221-223.

39. See Lyndon H. LaRouche, Jr., "The Science of Christian Economy," *op. cit.,* pp. 263-266; "On the Subject of God," *Fidelio,* Vol. II, No. 1, Spring 1993, pp. 24-33; and "History as Science: America 2000," *op. cit.,* pp. 60-64.

40. Man's existence in the solar system is measured relative to the surface of the planet Earth.

That is what is fairly described as my updated presentation of Leibniz's principles of a general theory of knowledge.

My argument on this point is summarily as follows.

IV. The Theory of Knowledge

The adequate solution to the paradox of negentropy lies within the domain of a theory of knowledge, an epistemology. We proceed to that as follows.

It is useful now to introduce the relevant, subsidiary argument, that perhaps the most notable feature of my work in this field is that these discoveries were not already established standard as textbook knowledge long prior to my initial, 1948-1952 work in this area. The shocking fact is, that such properly obvious consequences of Riemann's and Cantor's combined contributions were left to be adduced by one of my then modest qualifications in mathematics. Situate this point in the appropriate terms of reference: If one takes into account the most recent 550 years of science, especially the indispensable internal political history of science, the irony of my discoveries is crucially, and most instructively anomalous; it is not rightly considered to be mysterious.

Similar anomalies have appeared in the history of science in the circumstance that the discovery in question has been implicitly forbidden by some more or less intimidating imposition of false axiomatic assumptions upon established institutions of learning, such as commonplace classroom opinion. In my own case, the root of such false, but commonplace opinion is, of course, ultimately traceable to the Venetian neo-Aristotelians of the late-fifteenth and sixteenth centuries; but, the circumstance bearing directly upon the irony of my successes are to be traced to the more recent, special U.S.A. conditions arising in mid-twentieth-century teaching since around the close of the nineteenth century.

To illustrate the kind of argument required: The combination of London-directed,[41] French Jacobin

lunacy, and, later, conditions imposed by the 1814 Congress of Vienna, ended France's more than two centuries of supremacy in science and technology.[42] Similarly, Anglo-Saxon empiricism's subjugation of both the U.S.A. and continental European classrooms came about chiefly through the political hegemony institutionalized under the Versailles and later Yalta-Potsdam peace agreements. The same political logic applies to changes in Twentieth Century scientific opinion within the United States.

Until the close of the nineteenth century, at first French, and then, later, German world-leadership in science had been the standard of leading educational and governmental institutions. The cases of Bache[43]

---

41. At the time of the French Revolution, Jeremy Bentham (1748-1832) was employed by British East India Company executive and British Prime Minister Shelburne to run a "radical writers shop" at Shelburne's Bowood estate. Bentham and another East India Company operative, Samuel Romilly, penned many of the speeches that were delivered by Jacobins Marat and Danton during the height of the Paris revolt. It was essential for Shelburne and Bentham that the French republican, pro-American forces be crushed, and France be prevented from adopting a constitutional form of government modeled on the U.S. Constitution. Thus, while supporting the ultra-monarchist forces around Count Mirabeau, the British East India Company simultaneously provided covert financial aid to the Jacobins. Records of payments to Marat, Danton, and other Jacobin leaders are still on file at the British Museum.

42. The systematic destruction of France's *Ecole Polytechnique* is a leading example of how the Congress of Vienna's cultural policies were imposed. The *Ecole* had been the world's leading and most vigorous center of advancement of the physical sciences during the 1794-1814 period, under the leadership of its founder, the great Gaspard Monge. Through political intervention, Pierre Simon, Marquis de LaPlace and LaPlace's *protégé* Augustin Cauchy were assigned to destroy the *Ecole's* instructional program, exemplified in the notorious cases of Niels Heinrik Abel and Evariste Galois, both of whose work was first suppressed and then plagiarized, following the victims' early deaths. LaPlace's first act in this démarché was to organize the expulsion of Monge. Despite the continued, if much reduced, influence of the collaborators of Monge and Lazare Carnot in France, French science slipped rapidly from its preeminent position worldwide, to a poor second, as Germany's scientific ascendency emerged under the tutelage of the Humboldt brothers and leadership of circles associated with Carl Gauss during the 1820's. See Felix Klein, *Development of Mathematics in the Nineteenth Century*, trans. by M. Ackerman (Brookline, Mass.: Math Science Press, 1979); see also E.T. Bell, *Men of Mathematics* (New York: Simon & Schuster, 1937).

43. Alexander Dallas Bache (1806-1867), a brilliant graduate of West Point, carried the prestigious name and tradition of his great-grandfather Benjamin Franklin. During the 1820's and 1830's, nationalist strategists in Franklin's old Philadelphia political machine (led by Nicholas Biddle, the president of the Bank of the United States, publisher Mathew Carey, and German emigré economist Friedrich List) successfully organized the initial industrialization of the U.S. In 1837, Biddle sent Bache to Europe to work with scientists and educational leaders, including Carl Gauss, Wilhelm Weber, and Alexander von Humboldt. Back in the U.S., Bache formed a patriotic group of the best American scientists, known as the "*Lazzaroni*" (Italian for "beggars"), in close cooperation with the German and allied French scientists. Bache's group designed and organized the U.S. Naval Academy. As head of the U.S. Coast and Geodetic Survey, Bache was chief strategist for the emergence of an advanced U.S. military-industrial capability, and was a leading advisor on intelligence to President Abraham Lincoln.

and Agassiz[44] are illustrative of the influence of Gauss in particular.[45] At the turn of this century there occurred the onset of a sweeping change, toward radical empiricism in the cultural paradigms of relevant U.S. institutions. The concurrence of President Eliot at Harvard University, of Jim Crow law, and the nearly successive U.S. presidencies of Confederacy admirers Theodore Roosevelt and Woodrow Wilson, were all cut from the same piece of treasonous political cloth. The patriotic, economic-protectionist tradition of Washington, Monroe, Adams, and Lincoln was supplanted once again by the "free trade" and related dogmas of those presidents upon whom Britain's villainous Lord Palmerston had most relied, Pierce and Buchanan. At the onset of the century, William James and the British Fabian Society's John Dewey had been unleashed to ruin U.S. public education. Gradually, scientists in the Bache tradition, such as Chicago's Harkins,[46] were supplanted, at least in large degree, by a dominant role of increasingly radical expressions of empiricism.

These changes in culture fostered corresponding effects in the teaching and practice of science, of political economy, of philosophy, and of history within the world's increasingly hegemonic, Anglo-Saxon Establishment institutions. That politically aversive indoctrination of most among the elites of the world's nations trickled down to its effects upon the opinion-shaping in the classrooms, and among the populations generally.

The specific relevance of this for the case at hand is signalled by comparing this twentieth century imperial rise of empiricism to a related *pogrom* against Georg Cantor by the cronies of Leopold Kronecker.[47] That shameful political lynching of Cantor was a correlative of the same empiricist mob's malice shown so prominently by Bertrand Russell and other members of the Cambridge Apostles in their continuation of the earlier efforts of Kelvin, Helmholz, Maxwell, and Rayleigh to bury the principal achievements of Riemann, Weber, and Weierstrass.[48]

But for such specific historical circumstances, all that which is in my original contributions would have been well established knowledge long before my initial work of 1948-1952. Consequently, my role has resembled that of the rude little boy in Hans Christian Andersen's celebrated tale of "The Emperor's New Suit of Clothes." Beginning 1948-1952, I worked to fill a

---

44. Louis Agassiz (1807-1873), leading zoologist and geologist of the nineteenth century; and one of the greatest naturalists of all time. He was born in Switzerland, trained in Germany at the University of Erlangen, and later worked with the leading French naturalist, Cuvier. In 1846, Agassiz moved to the United States and, as chief professor of the Harvard Lawrence Scientific School, he become a leading member of Alexander Dallas Bache's "*Lazzaroni.*" Together with Admiral Charles Henry Davis, Bache, and Joseph Henry, Agassiz helped found the U.S. National Academy of Sciences in 1863. See his *Contributions to the Natural History of the United States* (Boston: Little, Brown & Co., 1857-62; reprint New York: Arno Press, 1978).

45. The U.S. Coast and Geodetic Survey began operation in 1817 as a branch of the Treasury Department, and was the only Federal government scientific agency during the first part of the nineteenth century. It was directed by F. Hassler until his death in 1843, after which Alexander Dallas Bache assumed its direction. Hassler carried on an extensive correspondence with Carl Gauss, who provided both scientific advice and equipment, continuing to advise the Coast Survey under Bache. In fact, most of Bache's leading assistants were either students or correspondents with Gauss. For example, Benjamin Peirce, who took over after Bache died in 1867, was a leading student of Gauss; Admiral Charles Henry Davis translated Gauss' book on the determination of celestial orbits. See Carl Friedrich Gauss, *Briefen und Gesprächen,* ed. by Kurt-R. Biermann (Munich: C.H. Beck, 1990).

46. William Draper Harkins (1873-1951), professor of physical chemistry at the University of Chicago for almost forty years. His students and laboratory equipment, such as the Chicago Cyclotron, made the success of the World War II Manhattan Project possible. See biographical introduction by T.J. Young to Draper's *The Physical Chemistry of Surface Films* (New York: Reinhold, 1952). Young points out that Harkins and E.D. Wilson published the first calculation for nuclear fusion of hydrogen to form helium in 1915. And, in the early 1920's, Harkins, together with Gans and Newson, was the first to generate and detect the formation of an excited nucleus, (Nitrogen-16) in a Wilson Cloud Chamber, "which may be regarded as the first radioactive element produced artificially."

47. Leopold Kronecker (1823-1891), professor of mathematics at the University of Berlin, politically dominated German mathematics during the 1870's and 1880's. A radical empiricist, he believed that integers alone had a basis in reality, and that all other numbers (e.g., irrationals) were figments of man's imagination; hence, Cantor's development of transfinite numbers was seen by Kronecker as a direct threat to his entire theory of mathematics. As early as 1874 Kronecker tried to block publication of Cantor's preliminary work on the non-denumerability of real numbers. Using his political influence, Kronecker threatened the editors of professional journals against publishing Cantor's work, which he denounced as "humbug"—a slander which, coming from so prominent a figure, had a particularly pernicious influence. Kronecker used his influence to prevent Cantor's appointment to a professorship at Berlin or Göttingen, relegating Cantor to a post at Halle, where he was physically isolated and financially impoverished. The strain of intellectual isolation and Kronecker's constant hounding contributed to the nervous collapse suffered by Cantor in this period.

48. See Bertrand Russell, *An Essay on the Foundations of Geometry* (1897) (New York: Dover Publications, 1956); also "On Some Difficulties in the Theory of Transfinite Numbers and Order Types," *Proc. London Math. Soc.* 4, 29-53, 1907. Russell's collaboration with Alfred North Whitehead in the composition of their notorious *Principia Mathematica* was a desperate effort to refute Georg Cantor's *Beiträge* by limiting mathematics axiomatically to the crudest possible forms of *analysis situs,* those of greater than, less than.

vacuum which had been created almost solely through a pervasive, political corruption of prevailing classroom opinion.

In this circumstance, looking at that retrospectively today, what I did was to extend what I had learned from the hand of Leibniz, to meet the challenge of refuting Wiener's "information theory." By aid of re-reading Riemann's dissertation through the transfinite eyes of Cantor, I developed a fresh overview of the theory of knowledge. This fresh overview, on which I report now, was required to resolve the remaining paradoxes posed by my locating of negentropy *elementarily* within the higher domain of the ontologically transfinite.

What is now to be said here may be read in part as parallel to Leibniz's 1695 "Système Nouveau de la Nature."[49]

The neo-Aristotelian system of deductive sense-certainty, as introduced to the sixteenth century by the gnostic Venetian associates of Gasparo Contarini,[50] is self-obliged by its own formalities to reduce everything to some smallest, discrete, finite, elementary particles. This system regards sense-impressions as virtually mirror-images of a reality outside our skins. Within such a linear materialist system, as for Aristotle himself, neither an intelligible notion of creation, nor of living processes, is logically possible; entropy rules always, everywhere. Formally, for Aristotle, his own existence is, speaking formally, like Newton's "Clock-Winder" universe, a logical-mathematical impossibility. If, according to his own system, the historical Aristotle ever existed, that would be sufficient proof that his system had no right to exist. If the prescribed system of knowledge implicitly prohibits the existence of the knower, that system has no right to exist.

The remedy for this fallacy of Aristotle's system was already defined by Plato before the completion of Aristotle's own studies at the Athens School of Rhetoric, the latter headed by the Sophist Isocrates. Negatively, in the sense of Plato's dialectical method of Socratic negation, we can demonstrate rigorously the necessity for the ontological elementarity of negentropy, i.e., for the Platonic elementarity of Heraclitus' notion of universal change. We can also represent this by means of a rigorously Platonic approach to use of constructive geometry, as Cusa thus treated the paradox of Archimedean quadrature. However, we cannot show this positively by means of any among today's generally accepted forms of classroom mathematics; this difficulty is, once again, an echo of Newton's "Clock-Winder" paradox.

We cannot render this notion of negentropic elementarity intelligible from the standpoint of sense-certainty. That is key to the formal fallacy permeating that Boltzmann theorem employed by Norbert Wiener's "information theory": that is also the form of the sundry kindred blunders of John Von Neumann, on economy and the human mind.

By means of what faculty can we overcome such paradoxes? Plato provided the general approach needed, but an adequate solution can be achieved only from the standpoint of the Leibniz science of physical economy. The contributions of Cantor, Riemann, and so on, were indispensable, Platonic steps toward my solution of the crucial, relevant issues of an intelligible theory of knowledge; but, *until these preliminary results were situated within the domain of physical economy, no adequate proof of the principles of knowledge is accessible.*

The form of this required solution is indicated by treating this issue in first approximation in its aspect as a problem in physics. A valid axiomatic-revolutionary discovery in natural philosophy is expressed, as customary, in the form of one or more crucial-experimental designs, experiments which demonstrate the principle of the discovery, each in a crucial way. Each such successful design, adequately refined, supplies a new principle to be incorporated usefully in either sundry machine-tool designs, or some similar use. The application

---

49. See G.W. Leibniz, "Système nouveau de la nature et de la communication des substances" (1695); English trans. "A new system of the nature and the communication of substances," in *Gottfried Wilhelm Leibniz: Philsophical Papers and Letters, op. cit.,* vol. II, p. 739. See also in *G.W. Leibniz: Mathematische Schriften,* ed. by C.I. Gerhardt (Berlin and Halle: 1849-1863; reprinted Hildesheim: 1962), vol. IV, p. 477.

50. Pietro Pomponazzi lectured on Aristotle at the University of Padua between 1487 and 1509, as well as at Ferrara and Bologna. One of his students was Gasparo (Cardinal) Contarini (1483-1542), a descendant of the Venetian oligarchical family, who became the most important Venetian operative during the period of the Protestant Reformation and the initial Catholic Counter-Reformation. Another influence on the young Contarini was Francesco Zorzi (Giorgi), who became his close friend. Among Contarini's close associates were Gregorio Cortese, the Abbot of the Benedictine Monastery of San Giorgio Maggiore, Reginald Cardinal Pole, a sometime-pretender to the English throne, and Gianpietro Caraffa, later Pope Paul IV. Pole and his friend Vittoria Colonna were central figures of the Italian crypto-Protestant movement called the "Spirituali." In 1537, Cardinal Contarini chaired the Holy See's Council on the Reform of the Church, which issued a decree citing Aristotle and condemning Erasmus, thus initiating the process leading to the Council of Trent.

of such designs, accompanied by the transmission of the corresponding new knowledge, expressed as use of improved tools of production, improved products, and so on, results in an increase in the physical productive powers of labor, *per capita* and *per* square kilometer. In other words, an increase in the potential population-density of mankind.

So, the continued successful existence of mankind[51] relies upon the mental processes which generate and replicate valid, newly-discovered, axiomatic-revolutionary changes in scientific and related knowledge. It is by adopting such manifestly creative states of mind, instead of naive sense-certainties, as the subject of conscious reflection, that we may access the pathway leading to the required theory of knowledge. This policy was the pivotal conception which emerged during my inquiries of the 1948-1952 interval, guiding me to my conclusions, through the pathways of Cantor and Riemann.

This emerging overview of the most crucial problem to be solved, prompted me to turn my earlier notions of geometry upside-down. Rather than build up a geometry, by extension, from primitive, linear sorts of axiomatic formal and ontological assumptions, take the reverse course. That which efficiently bounds externally as the relative macrocosm, is to be seen as the relatively elementary. It is the whole so defined which determines the part. This supplied me a corrected notion of the statement: "The whole is always greater than the sum of its parts." This view of the axiomatic structure of geometry-in-general freed my conscience from any further reliance upon accepted forms of classroom mathematics.

The realization that, axiomatically, none of the relevant epistemological paradoxes I was facing could find a model representation in terms of any presently accepted notion of a theory of functions, forced me to focus upon the internal history of mathematical physics, in search of some notion of an ordering-principle among axiomatic-revolutionary discoveries. The obvious place to begin a first attempt is the discovery addressed inclusively, and crucially, in Riemann's habilitation dissertation, the famous, ubiquitous theorem of Pythagoras. After all, obviously, the thirteen books of the *Elements*[52] bring the student from reconstructing that theorem, through, step by step, to Plato's five regu-

lar solids inscribed within a sphere. Give up those ordinary notions of denumerable ordering central to all algebraic and transcendental functions; seek a more modest notion of necessary ordering. For every axiomatic-revolutionary discovery, certain other such discoveries are necessary predecessor, and every valid such discovery is a necessary successor of others. Every professionally qualified teacher of mathematical physics employs that guiding notion in constructing efficient lesson-plans.

This approach to, implicitly, teaching mathematics and physics, shifts the focus from learning theorems and their formal proofs, to replicating in the student's mind the experience of each crucial, original axiomatic-revolutionary discovery as this occurred, in essence, in the original case, in the mind of the putatively original discoverer. Instead of treating theorems as the principal subject, make the subject the process of axiomatic-revolutionary discovery as replicably experienced by the student in each case. Make that moment of *Platonic hypothesis-formation* the subject.

Then, next, find the ordering-principle—the Cantorian *equivalence, type*—among a series of such successful acts of hypothesis-formation. Determine, according to such an adduced equivalence, the *type* of ordering of a network-sequence of such hypotheses according to the rule of "necessary predecessor"/"necessary successor."

The following step must be to render that adduced ordering-principle, that *type,* the intelligible subject of conscious comprehension. This is done, in first approximation, by contrasting this scientific method, as a Platonic method, to Aristotelian formalism. The recognition of the incurable fallacy of all Aristotelian and analogous argument, from this standpoint, is the beginning of a true epistemological insight into the required principles governing a scientific method.

That view of the *type* of ordered hypotheses, is rendering the higher hypothesis an intelligible subject of conscious comprehension, in turn. It is at this stage of the process of inquiry, that the crucial features of my definition of negentropy become adequately intelligible; the essential paradox is thus solved.

Reconsider the steps just described.

In a preliminary way, this pedagogical approach to the internal history of science has a well-established basis in Christian Classical humanist secondary education. The case of Groote's Brothers of the Common Life, and, later the Schiller-Humboldt educational re-

---

51. LaRouche, "Science of Christian Economy," *op. cit.,* pp. 241-256.
52. *The Thirteen Books of Euclid's Elements,* trans. by Thomas L. Heath (1925) (New York: Dover Publications, 1956).

forms, are obvious references.[53] These great Christian humanist educational reforms were reflected also, if in a diluted way, in the later examples of pre-1970, pre-catastrophe, U.S. secondary education.[54] In the better schools, as reflected in traditional professional scientific practice still, the student comes to know an axiomatic-revolutionary, or related discovery of principle by both its approximate date of occurrence, and the personal name (plus a short biographical sketch, perhaps) of the discoverer. I emphasize: that discoverer as an individual thinking person, whose discovery today's student can master only by replicating the mental process of discovery which occurred in that historic moment of discovery by the original discoverer.

As already noted, a teacher's good lesson-plan must reflect some degree of insight into the matter of arranging topics of principle according to "necessary predecessor"/"necessary successor." The crucial difference of emphasis proposed, relative to such established classroom precedents, is to shift the emphasis from getting to the accepted proof of the theorem, to concentration upon the internal features of the mental process of formulating the relevant hypothesis.

Thus, to each valid, axiomatic-revolutionary discovery assign the name of *hypothesis.* As said above, assign to the idea of an *equivalence* in ordering of necessary successive hypotheses, an *higher hypothesis.*

In the classroom, and here, too, the notion of hypothesis is brought into clearer focus, by contrasting hypothesis with the theorem-proofs of a formal, deductive theorem-lattice. In the latter case, every provable theorem of that more or less indefinitely expandable array will be deductively consistent with a set of axioms and postulates which underlies the initial germ-kernel of theorems of that lattice.

Let us denote such deductive consistency of formal theorem-lattices by a term borrowed from the customary usage of our adversaries, "hereditary principle."[55] Every possible theorem of a consistent theorem-lattice will be nothing but a reflection of the original body of "genetic material," the underlying set of axioms and postulates. The *Platonic hypothesis,* generated by the Platonic dialectical method of Socratic negation, overturns one or more of the axioms and postulates of any theorem-lattice of reference.

Thus, for the hereditary form of theorem-lattice, the theorem-proof of deductive consistency is the characteristic mental activity of the student. Once we introduce true discovery, and therefore *hypothesis,* theorem-proof is submerged; creative mental activity as such is everything. It is in this latter domain of conscious thought, and only here, that my notion of negentropy becomes adequately intelligible.

The challenge immediately presented at that juncture in our argument is the following: *If we abandon formal theorem-proof, as we must (since we are replacing axioms or postulates), what is the nature of proof of hypothesis?* The required proof has two fundamentally distinct aspects, two aspects which ultimately dissolve into one another, but not at first consideration.

For the student, the first kind of proof encountered is study of crucial discoveries from the past. Once that student has adduced a sense of the equivalence (higher hypothesis) of valid past discoveries of an axiomatic-revolutionary quality, the student's first resort, at each confronting of an unfamiliar such discovery, is to test that discovery for its quality of Cantorian *equivalence.*

Later, that student may acquire a second notion of proof, a proof rooted in the Leibnizian notion of a science of physical economy. If an hypothesis satisfies the standard of equivalence, and also increases implicitly humanity's potential population-density, it is *relatively valid.*

These two proofs merge into one historically. The equivalence among past discoveries (hypotheses) reflects the test of an implicit increase of mankind's potential population-density.

That is the general principle of the relevant theory of human knowledge, but only in one aspect, natural science.

<hr>

53. See Wilhelm von Humboldt, "Preliminary Thoughts on the Plan for the Establishment of the Municipal School System in Lithuania" and "School Plan for Königsberg," which are summarized by Marianna Wertz, in "Wilhelm von Humboldt's Classical Education Curriculum," *New Federalist,* Vol. VII, No. 10, March 15, 1993, p. 8; see also *Wilhelm von Humboldt, Humanist Without Portfolio: An Anthology of the Writings of Wilhelm von Humboldt,* trans. by Marianne Cowan (Detroit: Wayne State University Press, 1963). Humboldt's reform program was directly influenced by his long association with Friedrich Schiller. See "On Schiller and the Course of His Spiritual Development," by Wilhelm von Humboldt, and Schiller's "What Is, and To What End Do We Study, Universal History?" in *Friedrich Schiller, Poet of Freedom,* Vol. II, ed. by William F. Wertz, Jr. (Washington, D.C.: Schiller Institute, 1988).

54. See Carol White, "The Roots of British Radicalism," in *The New Dark Ages Conspiracy* (New York: New Benjamin Franklin House, 1980), pp. 285-333; see also "Origins of the Counterculture," in *Dope, Inc.: The Book That Drove Kissinger Crazy,* by the Editors of Executive Intelligence Review (Washington, D.C.: Executive Intelligence Review, 1992), pp. 533-553.

55. See, e.g., Bertrand Russell, *Introduction to Mathematical Philosophy* (1917) (New York: Simon & Schuster, Touchstone Books, 1971), p. 21.

This brings us to the last of the principal issues posed by Wiener's "information theory," to the subject of communication of ideas. We focus upon the idea of a language in its most general sense of a medium for communicable aspects of ideas. Within that setting, we treat the crucial special case of ideas which, by their nature, cannot be communicated literally. Consider the case for those ideas which correspond to Platonic hypothesis.

Since all ideas are subsumed by the notion of metaphorical communication of ideas of hypothesis, and, since language as a whole is bounded thus by those same principles, the notion of metaphorical provocation of hypothesis is the crucial case for all communication.

In the instance of every new Platonic hypothesis, language appears primarily as a mode of posing paradoxes to such effect that a speaker's new idea, which cannot be identified literally in existing language, can be replicated nonetheless in the mind of the hearer.[56] This leads us to the broader proposition, that *ideas* are not *primarily* sensual imageries, but are, *primarily, elementarily,* those valid, intelligible conceptions which cannot be named at first communication by a recognizable term of established usage. That is to say, that all valid ideas first appeared to existing language in no other form of communication but metaphor. Among such new ideas, the highest class, subsuming all other classes, is that of axiomatic-revolutionary ideas. Ideas of this class refer to a quality of sovereign mental activity within the speaker, an idea whose form is that of, variously, Platonic hypothesis, higher hypothesis, or hypothesizing the higher hypothesis. For reasons outlined above, all ideas were introduced to language first in the guise of metaphor. Then, and, even after many generations of use, those ideas were, and are still subject to those same functional notions of idea demonstrated by the case for Platonic hypothesis.

Perhaps the best illustration of metaphor, is the paradoxical quality of Plato's *Parmenides.* The same principle so shown by the *Parmenides,* is employed as the central feature of Nicolaus of Cusa's original solution to the ontological paradox of Archimedean quadra-

ture.[57] *The metaphor* is the ontologically required, indivisible concept which unifies a paradoxically juxtaposed set of predicates for the case the latter reflect the same function. For Plato's *Parmenides,* the indivisible *one* is always existent in *the ontological form of change,* Heraclitus's ontologically unique quality of *universally elementary change.* The form of this change may be compared to Cantor's principle of transfinite *equivalence*; for Cantor's mathematics, Heraclitus's *change* is the highest *type* in Plato's universal *Becoming.* In Cusa's titles *De Docta Ignorantia*[58] and "De Circuli Quadratura,"[59] the passage from the "Parmenides paradox," of an endless series of regular polygons, to the circular perimeter as an ontologically higher form of an axiomatic existence, is characterized by a shift from Euclidean space, to the higher, non-algebraic domain of space-time; the axiomatic *least-action, or isoperimetric* definition of the circle is closed *action* expressing a constant change, and *equivalence,* a higher *type* than formal Euclidean geometry, or algebra.

In both cases, Plato's *Parmenides* and Cusa's axiomatic-revolutionary treatment of quadrature, we are presented with examples of a true metaphor in approximately the barest-bones form of representation. *Cusa's non-algebraic generation of the circle, as constant change, is the metaphor represented by Archimedean quadrature.* That circle's existence cannot be competently defined in the axiomatic framework of ordinary Euclidean geometry; to construct a circle, we must employ a ruse of construction excluded from the underlying set of axioms and postulates of Euclidean theorem-lattice. We must employ *rotation,* as one does by drawing the circle with a compass. Rotation is the ordering of *action* in *non-algebraic space-time,* not Euclidean space.

This cannot be brushed aside with the argument that I am stretching a point here. There is a four-hundred-fifty year, connected historical development, from the origin of Cusa's discovery, through Leonardo da Vinci, Kepler, Fermat, Huygens, Leibniz, Bernoulli, and then to Hermite, *et al.* at the close of the nineteenth century, to define rigorously the transcendental distinction of π.[60] It is often, that proverbial, smug hand-waving at the

---

56. This incidentally, is the proper standpoint from which to appreciate the non-mysterious implications of Kurt Gödel's famous treatment of formally undecidable propositions (see footnote 26).

57. Note both the treatment of the circle in Nicolaus of Cusa's *De Docta Ignorantia* earlier and then, later, the summation of that in "De Circuli Quadratura" (see footnotes 16 and 17).

58. Nicolaus of Cusa, *De Docta Ignorantia, op. cit.*

59. *Ibid.*

60. See Ernest Shapiro, Leibniz from LaRouche's Standpoint, *EIR,* Aug. 4, 2017, p. 58.

blackboard is employed to evade even the most devastatingly crucial issues. Such has been the long, stubborn refusal to acknowledge that rotation is, axiomatically, ontologically external to a formal Euclidean theorem-lattice, or, as Augustin Cauchy's calculus has often been read to evade, the truth is that asymptotic limits are not theorems of the theorem-lattice employed to describe the relevant function.

All formal language, such as a grammatically literate spoken language, is laden with equivalent axiomatically ontological limits. Thus, contrary to the nominalists, all important ideas are introduced to a subsequent state of communicable recognition by means of initially metaphorical identification.

Those were the considerations, although more crudely formulated at the time, which obliged me to include in my 1948-1952 work on negentropy a corresponding treatment of the principal characteristics of metaphor in communication. For the purpose of this study, I chose then musical settings of poetry which had been composed during the 1780-1900 interval. The composers selected were chiefly Mozart, Beethoven, Schubert, Schumann, Loewe, Brahms, and Hugo Wolf. The central sub-topic of this study was two or more alternative musical settings of the same poem. The poets upon whom I concentrated were Goethe and Heine. The focus was upon the use of musical forms of metaphor in relationship to the natural musical vocalization in hearing and the poetic enunciation of the spoken line.

Later, beginning 1982, at my urging, aspects of my 1952 results were reconstructed with improvements by some of my musician associates. The latter study, of the 1982-1991 interval, is reported in the recently published Book I of *A Manual on the Rudiments of Tuning and Registration.*[61] The object of both this latter and the original study was to show the connection between creativity *per se*'s expressions in both the domain of natural philosophy and Classical art-forms. To treat the implications of negentropy for communications in general, thus to refute "information theory" adequately, it was necessary to demonstrate a relevant degree of *equivalence* of creativity *per se* in one medium to that in the other.

As I have identified this recently in "History as Science,"[62] the case of the Indo-European language family shows language in general to be premised centrally upon three elements.

First, the spoken language as typified by reading Classic Vedic hymns and Sanskrit from the standpoint of philologist Panini.[63] This working assumption of the 1948-1952 period was referenced then chiefly to the Classical English-language poetry, from Shakespeare through Shelley and Keats. Years later, the argument was given a selected crucial test against the Italian of Dante Alighieri's *Commedia.*

Second, the visual space-time field of geometry. This correlates with the most essential feature of spoken action, the transitive verb. By this use of the verb, we are able to locate qualities of transformation in space-time.

Third, music. All spoken language is governed by musical principles, even in the rudest of violations of those principles.[64] The application of this to choral singing among naturally determined different species of singing voices is again *bel canto polyphony. Bel canto polyphony* determines faultlessly a well-tempered tuning of the temper used by Bach, Mozart, Beethoven. This is determined by the natural harmonics of the biological speaking and singing apparatus of human beings all as members of but a single species. Thus, the system of well-tempered, Classical,[65] *bel canto* polyphony was not an historical accident of taste preferred only by some people, in some time and place. This was the musical medium implicitly ordained by God; it is implicitly imbedded in the genotype common to all members of the human species, past and present. The same argument governs the principles of *vocalization* of a spoken form of language.[66] Music is derived from the natural vocalization of Classical forms of poetry, as the Vedic hymns typify this general case.

It should be interpolated here, as a relevant point to be stressed. "Text" in the sense the term is used by "Deconstructionists" such as Jacques Derrida, does not—

---

61. See *A Manual on the Rudiments of Tuning and Registration,* ed. by John Sigerson and Kathy Wolfe (Washington, D.C., Schiller Institute, 1992), esp. chap. 11 *passim,* pp. 199-228. See also, Lyndon H. LaRouche, Jr., "Mozart's 1782-1786 Revolution in Music," *Fidelio,* Vol. I, No. 4, Winter 1992.

62. LaRouche, "History as Science," *op. cit.,* pp. 24-27.

63. Panini (c.400 b.c.), grammarian of Classical Sanskrit. P.B. Junnarkar's *An Introduction to Panini* (Baroda: Shanti S. Dighe, 1977) includes the full text of Panini's *Astadhyayi.*

64. *Cf. A Manual on Tuning, op. cit.,* chaps. 9 and 10, pp. 151-198. If the principle of least action is applied to voice training of singers, the result of this is a form of voice training associated with the *bel canto* tradition carved in stone by Luca della Robbia in the Cathedral of Santa Maria del Fiore in mid-Fifteenth Century Florence, Italy.

65. See *A Manual on Tuning,* pp. xv-xxix.

66. *Ibid.*

or, certainly should not—exist.[67] As the pagan god was reminded, his invention of writing was useful, with some potentially disastrous side-effects, of which Derrida is one. Written text should be heard by the writer and reader as it is being read, or written. The music—the vocalization of the spoken word, as shadowed on the written page—is an integral part of speech, as the geometry of space-time is also an integral part of speech, as Plato was first to show, as Leonardo da Vinci and Kepler later emphasized.

Fifty years ago the following point was not considered further than our present account has gone up to this moment. Even this much of the treatment of relevant musical matters so far, already includes some supporting material dating from times later than 1952. This, and the point now to be added respecting Plato's regular solids, are included here as they provide crucial supporting evidence for those conclusions respecting the theory of knowledge already reached, if on a narrower basis, forty years ago.

The Classical Greeks, who knew well-tempering in Plato's time,[68] recognized, more broadly, that natural beauty in art was characterized, in vision and in hearing, by harmonic orderings consonant with those of living processes. The whole design of the Classical Athens Acropolis attests to this.[69] Plato documents this.[70] Two key followers of Nicolaus of Cusa, Luca Pacioli and Leonardo da Vinci, demonstrate[71] that; Johannes Kepler bases the beginnings of a comprehensive mathematical physics upon the common harmonic characteristics of vision, music, and Plato's five regular solids. In modern language, this current in mathematical physics indicates Kepler to be the initiator (guided by Pacioli and da Vinci) of what is most fairly named today "quantum field theory."[72]

We are speaking of a theory of knowledge. We are gauging these queries against Riemann's referenced warning, on the subject of the metrical features of a continuous manifold. Thus: how can man come to know the crucial implications of the five Platonic solids? What is the nature of the available evidence on this matter? What was available to Plato's Classical Athens?

We have referenced the Acropolis. The Greeks knew the principles as artistic, and architectural proportions according to an harmonics of circular sections. They recognized, thus, as natural visual beauty harmonic orderings consonant with that Golden Section which is characteristic of Plato's five solids. This Golden Section-pivoted harmonics was recognized, as by da Vinci[73] and Kepler[74] later, as that characteristic which distinguished living from non-living processes. It is the metrical characteristic of actions governed by negentropy, as I defined negentropy, earlier here, and forty-odd years ago. The Golden Section was also recognized by Plato, for example,[75] as the characteristic of musical training. We have just considered the natural basis for that well-tempered system of *bel canto* polyphony, congruent with the Golden Section, which is implicitly determined by the human genotype. In short, vision and hearing are the imbedded metrical guides to our communicable forms of representation of our universe, in terms of the Golden Section's implications. Nonetheless, it is in the implicitly well-tempered underlay of the determination of a least-action mode of vocalized speech and singing, where lies the aspect of language in which this metrical principle of thinking is

67. See Webster G. Tarpley, "The Evil Philosophy Behind Political Correctness," *Fidelio,* Vol. II, No. 2, Summer 1993, pp. 42-54.

68. Aristoxenus (born c.375 b.c.), a student of the Pythagoreans and Aristotle, developed a fully-conceived system of musical tuning presented in such works as the surviving *Harmonic Elements,* whose "tense diatonic" scale has been interpreted by modern writers as containing a system of equal temperament. See *The Harmonics of Aristoxenus,* trans. and ed. by H.S. Macran (London: Oxford University Press, 1902); see also R. Westphal, *Aristoxenus von Tarent* (Leipzig: A. Abel, 1883-93; reprinted 1965).

69. See Pierre Beaudry, "The Acropolis of Athens: The Classical Idea of Beauty," *New Solidarity,* Vol. II, No. 24, June 24, 1988, pp. 6-7; see also, Lyndon H. LaRouche, Jr., "The Classical Idea: Natural and Artistic Beauty," *Fidelio,* Vol. I, No. 2, Spring 1992, p. 8ff.

70. See Plato, *Republic, op. cit.,* Steph. 509d-513e; *Timaeus,, op. cit.,* Steph. 32a, 35b-36b, 54d-55c.

71. See Luca Pacioli, *De Divina Proportione* (1497) (Vienna: 1896), whose geometrical diagrams of the Golden Section-determined regular solids were drawn by Leonardo da Vinci. Reproductions of these drawings appear in *The Unknown Leonardo,* ed. by Ladislao Reti (New York: McGraw-Hill Book Company, 1974), pp. 70-71.

72. This is not the place to take up the distinction between a so-called "quantum mechanics" and a "quantum field theory." It is sufficient to inform the reader that Planck's work leads as readily to a quantum field theory of quasi-Keplerian type, as to a strained quantum mechanics, and without the distressing paradoxes inhering in the latter. A point here is the theory of knowledge; only that implication is being treated in this part of the report.

73. See footnote 71. Leonardo's drawings and studies of plants and plant growth abound in the application of Golden Section harmonics.

74. See Johannes Kepler, *On the Six-Cornered Snowflake,* trans. by Colin Hardie (Oxford: Clarendon Press, 1966), reprinted by *21st Century Science & Technology,* 1991.

75. See Plato's *Timaeus* in *Plato: Timaeus, Critias, Cleitophon, Menexenus, Epistles,* Loeb Classical Library, trans. by R.G. Bury (Cambridge: Harvard University Press, 1929), Steph. pps. 32a, 35b-36b, 54d-55c.

imbedded. The well-tempered, *bel canto* polyphonic domain is the model for a quantum field, the model for a quantum-field conception of the metrical qualities of our physical space-time universe.

That leads directly to the principal point respecting a theory of knowledge.

Knowledge is accessible to mankind only in the forms corresponding to a theory of Cantorian *types,* in terms of hypothesis, higher hypothesis, and hypothesizing the higher hypothesis. We can know only *change,* the notion of universal elementarity of change which is associated with the writings of Heraclitus and Plato. That change is known to us in terms of *hypothesis,* or, in Cantor's terms, *types.*

However, the distinction between truthfulness and falsehood, respecting principles of nature, requires an experiment, an experiment which can be of but one *type,* physical economy as the practice of maintaining progress in increasing the potential population-density of mankind. This is uniquely the form of experiment which tests the relative validity of those choices of higher hypothesis (*types*) which govern the generation of those axiomatic-revolutionary discoveries which foster increase of potential population-density.

Thus, the popularized notion of "objective science" is so dangerously misleading that we must regard it as absurd, or even worse. Knowledge is *subjective,* in the sense that we must act upon principles of discovery which can be known to us only by proving their validity in practice in terms of the benefit to mankind as a whole, a benefit which is crucially centered upon the requirement of the continuing increase in the potential population- density of our species as a whole.

The source of our personal knowledge to this effect, is the reliving of history from this standpoint. The idea of a Christian Classical humanist education, such as that of Groote's Brothers of the Common Life, or the Schiller-Humboldt reforms, the reliving of moments of great, axiomatic-revolutionary discovery, as if to replicate that moment from within the mind of the original discoverer in one's own mind, is a typification of the relevant way in which the child and youth must be developed morally and formally at the same time.

By means of such an education, emphasizing the principles stated here, the mind of the child and youth, repeatedly experiencing the replication of valid axiomatic-revolutionary hypotheses in this way, is enabled to apply the same mental capacity, of hypothesizing, to the ordering ("necessary predecessor,"/"necessary successor"), the Cantorian equivalence of a series of valid hypotheses. Thus, this latter equivalence, or higher hypothesis, is the proper referent for the term *scientific method.* Since conflicting *scientific methods* may be compared by the same method of hypotheses, the student's mind is equipped, and thus impelled to enter into consciously hypothesizing the higher hypothesis.

This activity within the individual defines a self-critical capability in respect to all aspects of his or her individual practice, and to observing the manifest mental processes and characteristic practice of others, including entire nations and cultures, past, present, and prospective future. Thus, by this developed subjective mental discipline, which is the proper notion of the scientific faculty, the individual judges relative truth, relative falsehood, right and wrong, superior and inferior qualities, and kindred judgment of those qualities for which mere "matters of taste" are not to be tolerated by a people which prizes its own continued moral fitness to survive.

From this relative knowledge, we are assured of a few things of an essential practical importance respecting absolute matters.

For example, Cantor references this domain by equating his own *transfinite* to Plato's *Becoming,* and his *absolute* to Plato's *Good. Becoming* is *physical space-time,* in which development occurs through *change.* Absolute, or Good, is reflected in the process of Becoming, as a process of perfecting, conceived as a perfected instant, a *One,* everywhere more than co-extensive with the Becoming. That said, return to the Becoming, and to those notions which have a relatively changeless quality, relative to the marginal uncertainty of approximations.

Once we grasp the idea, that man is distinguished absolutely above all other living creatures, solely by our willful capacity for effecting voluntarily axiomatic-revolutionary improvements, increases in mankind's command over nature, that voluntary creative activity, the activity of *Platonic hypothesis,* that axiomatic-revolutionary activity, compared with the resulting change in man's *per-capita* power over nature, is the phenomenon to which all rational employment of the term "knowledge" is referenced.

It is not the observed relations among sense phenomena, which is the subject of knowledge. The proximate subject of knowledge is the *changes* in sensory phenomena's patterns of behavior which have been, are being effected cumultatively, historically, through the creative faculty of hypothesis generation. It is the relationship of such changes to increases in potential population-density, and to man's breaking through barriers of technology, to make richly habitable the deserts, or barren planets beyond our own, which test, historically to present date, those adducible principles of higher hypothesis which are thus shown to be the most reliable known choices of guides to truth respecting man's relationship to nature.

All along, there are certain virtually absolute social truths, with the moral force of *natural law,*[76] embedded in the cumulative evidence of historically successful, Platonic higher hypothesis.

First, the sacredness and lawful sovereignty of the individual person's life, by reason of that creative faculty expressed as Platonic hypothesis.

Second, the subsumed sacredness of the parental household, for its interdependent loving (*agapic*[77]) functions of procreation and nurture of new, individual personalities through the ages of infancy, childhood and youth, to blossoming as a young adult with developed creative powers.

Third, the derived sacredness and functions of those institutions we know as republics under *natural law,* those more powerful, less mortal agencies whose function is to defend the sacredness of individual creative life, to defend the institution of the parental household, and to foster and protect the benefits of creative individual work to the advantage of all present and future generations of mankind.

The Monad

We now come to certain concluding points of summation so crucially important, that I must set them somewhat apart from the immediately preceding pages of this concluding section. The first of these is my fresh proof of the *monad.*

Consider, from the standpoint of language as I have defined language: How do we know with the authority of necessary and sufficient reason, that man possesses an individual soul? It is most appropriate to state the case of the monad in that form, because for Gasparo Contarini's Aristotelian cronies, such as the exemplary Pomponazzi, for all consistent Aristotelians, the individual soul could not exist. Thus, for all empiricists, and other neo-Aristotelians, the individual soul does not exist, but rather a "bolshevik," e.g., a "collective soul." For whomever rejects the notion of Platonic hypothesis, the individual soul cannot exist; that is the functional connection I am stressing here.

Turn to our earlier treatment of the subject of metaphor.[78]

Any idea, in its guise either as an original discovery, or in its transmission *de novo* as it might have been an original discovery, cannot be transmitted as a literal intent of the language-medium employed, but only as the intent which reposes in the individual user of that language. The idea cannot be addressed by any formal analysis of the language-medium employed. This predicament is a consequence of the fact that any true discovery corresponds to a formally absolute discontinuity in any system of deductive representation previously employed. Relative to language as such, true ideas lie only in the individual, creative mental processes of each person participating in the communication.

This illustrates, and also demonstrates implicitly the relationship between a true, i.e., negentropic continuous manifold and individual existence of the form shown as the originally metaphorical character of all communicated ideas. The truth on this point has been right under everyone's nose for millennia past. Here lies the kernel of Leibniz's *Monadology,* and my own. Here lies the key to exposure of a *politically corrupted* Leonhard Euler's perversely falsified attack upon Leibniz's *Monadology.*[79] The crucial point here is this; no idea corresponding to a Platonic hypothesis may be communicated to another person except as metaphor; no language can explicitly, literally transmit a true idea. Ideas are transmitted by aid of use of language, but this in a manner comparable to the common features of Plato's *Parmenides* and Cusa's solution for the paradox of quadrature. *Ideas* do not exist among individuals, but only within individuals. They exist within individuals only by being generated *de novo* within each person. They may be communicated only by use of paradox, i.e., metaphor, to provoke the replication of the original generation of the idea within, and by means of the sovereignly individual creative mental, hypothesis-generating processes of that individual person.

---

76. This pertains to the intelligibility of principles of higher hypothesis by creative reason. On natural law generally, see G.W. Leibniz. Natural law signifies those universal, endurable principles of the world as Becoming which are naturally intelligible to individual creative reason. For example, as given in the text, the principle of the sacredness of the individual person, the derived sacredness of the family, and the derived relative sacredness of the republic form of government.

77. The term "agapic" signifies the agapic form of love in opposition to erotic love. The reference is, of course, to the *Gospel of St. John,* especially the famous verse 3:16, and to *I Corinthians* 13 of St. Paul, as the standard for defining *agapē.*

78. Lyndon H. LaRouche, Jr., "On the Subject of Metaphor," *op. cit.,* pp. 20-26.

79. G.W. Leibniz, *Monadology, op. cit.*

That shows us the following. By virtue of the creative-mental, hypothesis-generating processes of the person, *each and all persons are singularities within, of the physical space-time domain.* They are *higher monads.* That point is crucial. This next is also crucial.

The form of both higher hypothesis, and hypothesizing the higher hypothesis, is the form of negentropy as I have defined negentropy in opposition to Wiener *et al.* Thus, to take higher hypothesis as a subject of conscious reflection is to be conscious of this form of negentropy *as an object of conscious thought,* a *thought-object.*[80]

This next is also crucial, similarly.

Also, that which defines the individual person as having intelligibly a personal soul, is the principle of Platonic hypothesis. To wit: the reason Aristotelians could never solve, or even comprehend the *Parmenides* paradox is not only that the joke against the Eleatics is equally applicable to Aristotle and to Sophists generally. The reason no language could communicate ideas literally is that ideas are generated by functions of discontinuities, that ideas are characteristically of the domain of higher transfinite types. This is the characteristic of negentropy; this is also the proof of the uniqueness of the individuality of the *monad,* of the person.

This next, then, is also crucial.

The idea of a true continuum must be nothing other than a continuous function of hypothesis-generation, an higher hypothesis. That higher hypothesis must be of the characteristic form of negentropy, a form equivalent to the verb "to create."

This next crucial argument follows.

All true human knowledge is of the form of hypothesizing the higher hypothesis. Thus the forms of this process of generating knowledge are the forms equivalent to knowledge of the real world, that real world which is mankind *increasing its* per-capita *power over physical space-time.* That increasing is the equivalence of the higher hypothesis as itself a process. That process, taken as a subject of willful consciousness, is human knowledge, is *science* in the most comprehensive meaning of the term science since the work of Cusa and Leibniz.

Next, the crucial issue here: that which is elementary within the process of conscious knowledge, defined in this way, is the idea which corresponds to what is elementary in that transfinite universe of Becoming which lies outside our skins.

From the side of language which corresponds to ge-

ometry, metaphor addresses a universe which is *elementarily negentropic change.* This view of *elementarity,* opposite to that of the neo-Aristotelian materialists Bacon, Galileo, Newton, *et al.,* is the sure-footed advantage gained by shifting consciousness from obsessive fixation upon sense-certainties, to a consciously critical examination of those internal mental processes by means of which supposed, and real knowledge is generated. That is the shift from the blind, mystical materialist faith in the elementary particles of Democritus and Lucretius, to the elementary reality of change as such. This is a formal solution for the continuum paradox. Summarize that solution as follows. In place of simply a Platonic view of Heraclitus' "nothing is permanent but change," say "Nothing is permanent but change subsumed by continuing negentropic action," defining *negentropy* as I have defined it in opposition to the statistical vulgarization employed by modern, post-Mach positivists[81] such as Wiener and Von Neumann.

To restate the underlying, applicable argument from the domain of the theory of knowledge, *knowledge* is a term properly restricted in use to identify our own minds' conscious image of those of its own cognitive processes which, as a Cantorian *type,* account for the increase historically of man's increased power over nature, *per-capita* and *per-*square kilometer of our planet's surface.

This leaves one correlated topic of language to be considered at this juncture, the notion of the *quantum field,* as that notion is to be traced from Plato's treatment of the five Platonic solids, through the modern work of Pacioli,[82] da Vinci,[83] and Kepler.[84] The special

---

80. See LaRouche, "On the Subject of Metaphor," *op. cit.,* pps. 22-23, 44-47.

81. Ernst Mach (1838-1916) initiated the effort to impose positivism on science in the twentieth century, and is generally credited with founding the fraud known today as modern "philosophy of science." While most of his scientific conclusions have long been proven false— for example, "that atoms [don't] exist"—his general method, particularly his opposition to any notion of causality in science, have become prevalent in modern physics. Mach led a scientific vendetta against Ludwig Boltzmann—eventually leading to his suicide in 1906—because Boltzmann refused to completely abandon the concept of causality in thermodynamics. He afforded similar treatment to Louis de Broglie at the 1927 Fifth Solvay Conference on Physics, and later, to Erwin Schroedinger. De Broglie characterized these events as "a virtual *coup d'état* in theoretical physics." See Morris Levitt, "Linearity and Entropy, Ludwig Boltzmann and The Second Law of Thermodynamics," *Fusion Energy Foundation Newsletter,* Vol. II, No. 2, Sept. 1976, pp. 3-18; see also Uwe Parpart,"The Theoretical Impasse In Inertial Confinement Fusion," *Fusion,* Vol. III, No. 2, Nov. 1979, pp. 31-40.

82. See Luca Pacioli, *De Divina Proportione, op. cit.*

83. See footnote 73.

84. For Kepler's concept of the "quantum field," see his *Mysterium Cosmographicum* (The Secret of the Universe), trans. by A.M. Duncan (New York: Abaris Books, 1981); chap. 2 contains his explicit reference

connections to language now to be stressed here, is the fact that the principles of well-tempered polyphony were already natural principles of human speech and singing even before the first human language were developed. That is to say, implicitly, that this well-tempered quantum field is already a natural characteristic of the mental image of our speaking and hearing any spoken (or, sung) language. This heard characteristic of those language images correlates to such expressions as the Golden Section with the visual, i.e., geometric facet of language. In the field of vision, this notion of quantum field is also associated with the notion of qualities of color attributed uniquely to respectively partitioned sectors of an ostensibly continuously defined frequency-domain of the visible field. We may thus speak, in this sense, of innate ideas, ideas which appear to us as comprehensible, intelligible ideas only from that higher consciousness of our own conscious processes

which is Plato's hypothesizing the higher hypothesis.

Thus, the notions of *monad, negentropy,* and *quantum field* are innate ideas whose existence and nature are susceptible of being rendered intelligible to us, if we look at the use of language as a medium for generating those forms of metaphor needed to communicate valid, genuinely creative discoveries of principle by individual persons. If we employ the contributions of such figures as Plato, Cusa, Leibniz, and Cantor to assist us in making ourselves conscious of our own conscious processes, in terms of hypothesis, higher hypothesis, and hypothesizing the higher hypothesis these innate and related ideas are made intelligible to us.

To the degree the human creative processes have been educated, through aid of reliving original acts of creative discovery over a long span of history, to define higher hypothesis governing new discoveries of principle for human practice, that individual mind, seeing its own relevant conscious activity of hypothesis-generation in that way, in that context, is seeing there a mirror of the lawful universality of our universe in its aspect as Platonic *Becoming.* It is in that view of matters that proper notions of knowledge in general, and scientific principles more narrowly, are to be adduced.

---

to Nicolaus of Cusa. For Kepler's discussion of the Divine Proportion (Golden Section), and of the geometric determination of harmonic relations, both in music and astronomy, see his *Harmonice Mundi* (The Harmony of the World), in *Opera Omnia,* vol. 5, (Frankfurt: 1864); English trans.: Books I-IV, trans. by Christopher White, et al. (unpublished); Book V, trans. by Charles Glenn Wallis, included in *Great Books of the Western World* series (Chicago: Encyclopedia Britannica, 1952).